.2 Dec 2000

THE
MINDFLOW©
METHOD

THE
MINDFLOW©
METHOD

How You Can Achieve Anything by
Not-Wanting and Not-Doing

TOM MOEGELE

HAY HOUSE

Carlsbad, California • New York City
London • Sydney • New Delhi

Published in the United Kingdom by:
Hay House UK Ltd, The Sixth Floor, Watson House,
54 Baker Street, London W1U 7BU
Tel: +44 (0)20 3927 7290; Fax: +44 (0)20 3927 7291
www.hayhouse.co.uk

Published in the United States of America by:
Hay House Inc., PO Box 5100, Carlsbad, CA 92018-5100
Tel: (1) 760 431 7695 or (800) 654 5126
Fax: (1) 760 431 6948 or (800) 650 5115; www.hayhouse.com

Published in Australia by:
Hay House Australia Pty Ltd, 18/36 Ralph St, Alexandria NSW 2015
Tel: (61) 2 9669 4299; Fax: (61) 2 9669 4144; www.hayhouse.com.au

Published in India by:
Hay House Publishers India, Muskaan Complex,
Plot No.3, B-2, Vasant Kunj, New Delhi 110 070
Tel: (91) 11 4176 1620; Fax: (91) 11 4176 1630; www.hayhouse.co.in

Text © Tom Moegele, 2018, 2020

English language translation by Louise Burfitt, 2020

The moral rights of the author have been asserted.

The information given in this book should not be treated as a substitute
for professional medical advice; always consult a medical practitioner. Any
use of information in this book is at the reader's discretion and risk. Neither
the author nor the publisher can be held responsible for any loss, claim or
damage arising out of the use, or misuse, of the suggestions made, the
failure to take medical advice or for any material on third-party websites.

A catalogue record for this book is available from the British Library.

Tradepaper ISBN: 978-1-78817-454-1
E-book ISBN: 978-1-78817-460-2
Audiobook ISBN: 978-1-78817-564-7

Interior illustrations: part and chapter opener images: Shutterstock;
54, 119 icons: www.flaticon.com; all other illustrations by Susanne Lesser

MIX
Paper from
responsible sources
FSC
www.fsc.org   FSC® C013056

Printed and bound in Great Britain by
TJ Books Limited, Padstow, Cornwall

*When you let go of everything
and stop holding on,
then you will receive everything.*

CONTENTS

PREFACE

Dear readers,

During the past decades I've come to know and master many healing methods, modalities, and coaching approaches, and all have subsequently proved to be boring or long-winded. Tom Moegele's MindFlow Method was new to me, and like nothing I'd ever experienced before.

How could I achieve more in life by 'Not-Doing'? How could I use my 'energy blocks,' as well as those of other people, to become stronger and more powerful? It's here that an image occurs to me – that of a Qigong master being pushed by 10 people at once. The more people who push him, the more energy he gains and the more centered and powerful his stance becomes.

When Tom first told us about his system, I thought it sounded utopian and implausible. I couldn't imagine being able to change and improve the energy in a strained atmosphere purely through one's own internal stance and one's own state – or that one could gain even more energy as a result.

I couldn't imagine that a state of 'Not-Wanting' could lead us to the very place where our real destiny lies. I couldn't conceive the fact that blocks are nothing more than accumulated energy that can be quickly and quite easily brought back into flow, like a balloon burst with a needle. But I was brought to my senses. It's all so simple that it first requires us to understand and relearn this simplicity.

As a publisher, this concept was new for us, but it gradually became more and more accessible until we were able to pour it into a book as an intellectually sound system. When Tom works energetically, you can feel and read from people's faces that something is happening, and something is being resolved. This book presents an approach for diving into this work. The knowledge, exercises, and tools it contains will allow you to access the unique concept of MindFlow.

In February 2017, I accompanied Tom on his trip to India with a tour group of 45 participants, and witnessed as deep-seated blocks that had hindered people for years were released within minutes. I marveled as I spoke with the seminar participants about what Tom's work has done for them and how their lives have changed for the better as a result. You'll find their testimonials throughout the book.

One testimonial in particular has remained with me – that of Ursula, an elderly Swiss woman who spoke with me on the bus ride from Jaipur to Udaipur (*see page xiv*). She expressed the changes that have occurred in her life as a result of MindFlow with such emotional depth, authenticity, and honesty that her words still bring tears to my eyes today, just as they did for her that day.

We hope that you enjoy reading this book.

Bernhard Keller

Momanda Publishing

Testimonial
Ursula from Switzerland

I've been working with Tom for about two years, and I feel simply that I've 'arrived.' MindFlow impacts every area of life – from relationships to awareness – and it's the best feeling possible: like coming home to oneself. There's no more needing to want. Just *being*.

I've always known in my heart that this feeling exists, yet I experienced it only very rarely. And when you do then experience that feeling, and know how you can reconstruct it again and again – how you can return to it over and over – well, for me, that's 'arriving.' Having a better understanding of one's fellow humans as a result of this awareness is also such a blessing. No more needing to fight, or wanting to have something – just *being*. For me, that's the most intense part of it.

This incredible sense of arrival is the greatest gift that a person could ever give to me… showing me how to get there. [*She starts crying.*] There's nothing you can say to that. It's simply an indescribable gift. And knowing you can never lose it, and that you'll always have it with you, well, that's everything.

It is everything and nothing. The nothing is everything. I'd heard about this 'nothing,' this 'emptiness,' over and over again. But what is the emptiness? How does it feel? What is it like? MindFlow has shown me that when you feel it and you're in that state of consciousness, you no longer speak. You don't say anything at all. There's just infinite silence.

MY JOURNEY SO FAR

To describe how I developed the MindFlow Method, I have to start, strange as it may at first seem, in the early days of my childhood. MindFlow wasn't shaped by big milestones such as leaving school, achieving a university degree, or accepting a great job. Instead, it was shaped by the notes *between* the lines – the subliminal tones I've heard all my life.

But when I was very young, this was difficult to pin down. I wanted to use these tones to explain my surroundings in words, but no one understood until I found a translation for them. The MindFlow Method emerged from all these sounds and experiences.

BEGINNINGS

I was born in Germany on May 20, 1970 as a premature baby and spent the first eight weeks of my life in an incubator. It was a bumpy start, as you can imagine, and at the time nobody could have imagined that this beginning could be a gift for me.

Even in kindergarten I suspected that, compared to the other children with whom I had contact, there was something 'different' about me. I found the route to kindergarten itself extremely uncomfortable. It went right past a cemetery, where I perceived dark shadows and dark, heavy energies everywhere; I also saw how people living in the vicinity of the cemetery lost their life energy.

A photo from that time shows me in fancy dress costume at carnival time – the only crying child in the middle of a cheerful crowd of kids. After two months at kindergarten, my parents had to take me out because I couldn't process the events that were being 'gifted' to me on my way there. I was overwhelmed and, as a result, not as happy and carefree as the other children.

I clearly had capabilities that made family life and interactions with other people difficult for me. On the one hand, I was extraordinarily sensitive, and on the other hand, my thought processes were completely unlike those of other people. Therefore, I handled things in a different way to that usually expected from children or adolescents. My family was very challenged by the way I perceived and accepted things.

When I was young, I reported on situations and the people involved with total naivete; and I assessed them completely correctly without knowing it. One day I was out with my mother when we encountered a man who was close to death. I tugged on my mother's clothes and told her that this man was about to collapse due to health problems. A few minutes later, that was exactly what happened. The man collapsed before our eyes and was given medical attention.

My mother was frozen: I was four years old at the time. After several incidents like this, my family decided to seek help. Therapeutic assessment showed that I was completely normal, merely equipped with the gift of being 'highly sensitive.'

At the same time, at the ages of three and four, I enjoyed spending time with my great-uncle in his workplace – he ran an engineering office and a large construction company. A construction site was an environment in which other boys would probably have been particularly impressed by the power of the large diggers. For me, however, the best thing was handing over the wages to the employees every Friday. From them I felt fears, worries, joy, suffering, energy, manipulation, intrigue, and spite. Emotions and states that, of course, I wasn't familiar with at the time. But I observed how different people were.

Desiring a 'completely normal' child, my parents made another attempt to place me in kindergarten. This time, it was one run by Catholic nuns, who were very warm and had a lot of time for us children. They engaged with my 'gift,' and recognized in me not just a 'crazy' child but someone with a special talent, and I felt relatively comfortable at the school.

After a while, the head teacher made no secret of the fact that I was different from the other children. She already saw me as a future professor because what I said fundamentally made sense: I would think everything through before opening my mouth to make a clear statement.

Our family home in Bavaria was surrounded by the Spessart, a large contiguous oak forest, and as a youngster, I enjoyed spending the whole day in the great outdoors with five or six other children. We built tree houses and small huts between trees, to which we'd retreat. It was a feeling that I still love today: the power of nature, tranquility, and the certainty that there are truthful, pure, and absolute things – air, earth, silence, the forces of nature.

I especially liked the time before I started elementary school, when I was allowed to skip kindergarten and instead walk through the Spessart with my maternal grandfather and his friends, all pensioners. I learned a lot about nature and the energy in the forest. The older men deliberately sought out places of power in which to do their physical exercises, and they became pain-free as a result.

I perceived these high-energy places as bright spots – like very bright smoke or light flickering through the area, or transparent confetti sprayed into the air. Sometimes, instead of their sports exercises, the men played music together. Their joy and the good vibrations that resulted from this remain happy memories to me to this day.

I had completely different experiences with my paternal grandfather. His large farm was located in the forests around Augsburg and he was mainly concerned with investments – for him, everything revolved around money (one got the feeling that he may have invented Monopoly). He was not only interested in investing in large projects, but also loved winning money from playing Schafkopf, a traditional Bavarian card game.

As my grandfather soon realized that I could remember all the cards that had been played, he taught me the rules of the game. I was allowed to play with the adults or in a team with my grandfather, and whomever I played with won every round. The adults who benefited from it liked having me as a teammate.

From today's perspective, I'd say that the fact I could memorize the cards wasn't that important. Rather, it was that I could read the respective energies of those involved: whether the player was bluffing or whether they actually had good cards in their hand. The card game then became very simple. If a person had bad cards, they became dark and transparent; they 'walked away,' so to speak, as soon as they looked at their hand.

Those who had good cards became bright and present – they were quite literally radiant, even though there was no obvious emotion on their faces. If someone became 'less,' they had a bad hand; if someone became 'more,' I knew it was time to be careful. I can still look at poker players today and tell whether someone has good or bad cards.

Aside from card games and money, I also learned how to deal with animals from my paternal grandfather. Animals became nervous when approached, for example, by a vet, but somehow, I had a supernatural connection to them: I knew their needs and managed to calm them down. In order to do this, I touched their foreheads with my right hand. Although my two grandfathers were very different characters, they both nonetheless made a big contribution to the MindFlow Method in my youth.

MY UNDERCOVER LEARNING SYSTEM

When I started elementary school, I was confronted for the first time with rigid structures and those who implemented them. It gave me the creeps – inside me, everything bristled. As a result of its opposition to freedom, the laws of nature, and good energies, school was a bleak time for me. And so it wasn't long before I developed an optimized, personal learning system for dealing with it.

My excellent, almost photographic memory helped me to retain what I'd read in detail forever. I studied ahead in class so that I had a lot of time for wonderful energies in the afternoon. When the last lesson of the day was over, I explored life in the forest with my friends again or, in later years, devoted myself to sports.

At first, my 'undercover learning system' – in which I took little part in the actual school teaching process but did my own teaching – went unnoticed, so I thought it was the solution. The teachers even valued me when I was able to recite poems flawlessly at school events. I was able to memorize the poems after reading them just twice, and it was easy for me to recite them with the right intonation. This was how I survived elementary school.

In the third grade, along with other Catholic children my age, I was prepared for my First Holy Communion. Although I'm not looking to diminish the image of the Church, unfortunately, my own experiences are not sufficient to improve it. I quickly realized that it's not all roses in the Catholic Church – the priests lacked empathy, good communication, and the skills necessary to deal with children.

I tried to skip Communion classes as much as possible, which meant I was almost not allowed to take Communion. I owe it only to my mother's commitment to the Church that I did. And although I'd have liked to rebel against the Church after this celebration, as a nine-year-old in an arch-conservative Catholic household, I had no chance of avoiding Sunday church attendance.

What bothered me about going to church? We went to the building full of energy and left it low in energy. In church, people lose their grounding; their energy is taken away, and this makes them more susceptible to manipulation. I felt that I went in happily and came out in a bad mood; I became tired and had to try not to fall asleep in the pew, but I often dozed off. I'd been given a watch for my First Communion so I could keep track of the time. In one service, after exactly 45 minutes, I got up from the pew to go outside because I thought that was enough time for church; it caused quite a big fuss. Nevertheless, I can still remember the entire service word for word, including the liturgy.

In the fourth grade of elementary school, it was time for the high school entrance exams. During the language exam, we were required to compose a retelling of a story. As I'd enjoyed reading books throughout my childhood, large stacks of them had collected in my room. The evening before the exam, when I was about to be sent to bed, I 'coincidentally' picked up one of my books, opened a page and read the respective text. And as it happened, it was this very story that was put in front of us as part of the exam! My subconscious had already processed the content overnight and I was able to write an essay that was marked as 'Very Good.'

It was the same with the math exam. The day before, I had the idea of doing a specific task, and it was this very calculation that ended up being part of the test. So nothing stood in the way of my moving up to a good high school.

However, high school was a challenge for me. As a young man with the ability to quickly assess other people, I increasingly experienced problems with my teachers. This was mostly because I was unable to accept them as authority figures because of their human shortcomings. I couldn't help but perceive the respective teacher along with all their fears and issues. Yet I also didn't know how to turn off this filter.

I have to admit, I was a little desperate at the time and tried to numb myself by playing sports. My afternoons were crammed with tennis matches that were supposed to make me so tired and devoid of feeling that the daily stories of my surroundings disappeared completely. I felt this reality show ought finally to come to an end – I didn't *want* to know everything, and I fought against it. Was I a victim? Yes, maybe I was at that time, because I couldn't defend myself against the flood of information.

My tried-and-tested elementary school teaching system was still working, but the day came when a teacher decided that from then on I'd have to do my homework at home in the afternoon, like all other children. A message was sent to my parents... and my world was destroyed. How dare the teacher do that?! I was a little bit hurt and chose confrontation. Without knowing the powers I had, I began my revolt. You don't want to know all that I learned in school... but it had everything to do with MindFlow.

COPING WITH STRUCTURE

All told, I got a good high school diploma without really having to make an effort. After graduating, I proceeded on to military service. My father had described the drill in the military as extremely taxing; essentially, we would be polished. I was already familiar with these structures from school, so it felt similar, just a little more crusty. I made the best of it and studied the interpersonal relationships at all levels within the armed forces. It was an exciting time which showed me that my skills would also be useful.

Military service was followed by a six-month stint abroad in France – as someone with very little understanding of French, I was just looking for a challenge. I was based in the Alps, above the tree line, supervising international groups as a ski instructor. As I don't come from the Alps, I wasn't as good at skiing as the locals, but I was able to assess my participants very well and teach them a lot, as I'd had to teach myself to ski a short time previously.

I was supposed to teach a snowboard course, too, although I'd never stood on such a board before. So my boss handed me a snowboard and I headed to the top of the highest mountain with it under my arm. I had an afternoon to learn to snowboard. As a skier, I wasn't afraid of speed and got down to business without fear. There were still a few snowboarders out that afternoon, and as I settled into it I basically 'copied' what they were doing. This allowed me to do the same moves and I found I had the necessary balance. Basically, I became those whom I was imitating.

It was about 30 minutes before I could snowboard down the mountain. The next day, because I'd only just learned snowboarding myself, I was able to explain to the participants how the appropriate movements *felt*. In retrospect, I can say that I learned to snowboard in an energetic way.

Following the winter in France, I completed a placement as part of my engineering degree course and learned how to use steel irons, files, and welding equipment in a training workshop. In line with one of the foreman's ideas, we were to square off a round steel base by hand using a file. Two weeks were allocated for this task and boredom was inevitable.

After two days I felt such enormous aggression against the file and the steel that my file broke apart in the middle without any further assistance. In his 30-year career, the horrified foreman had never seen anyone cut the steel file in two before. My anger at being bullied had given rise to an unexpected strength that I'd previously felt at my school desk.

My perceptions became clearer and sharper with increasing age and knowledge, and there were phases when it was impossible for me to go into the city or to large events. When I was younger it had been the teachers whose issues I could read, along with smaller groups of young people, relatives, and friends. However, at a big event like a concert, or in a big city, there were suddenly thousands of people whose lives I could immerse myself in. A mass of information appeared to me, completely unfiltered.

I loved the opera, but could no longer go to the theatre because I threatened to melt away in my suit – beads of sweat formed on my forehead. As you can imagine, it was not just good news that featured among all this information I was receiving. This was the peak of what I'd experienced so far in connection with my so-called 'gift.' I didn't want to be able to read other people's lives! And for that reason, I preferred to live a solitary life myself.

A little later I realized that isolating myself socially wasn't the answer, so life forced me to work out my solution. It was another milestone on the way to my MindFlow Method. During my years of study, I took it upon myself to search all the esoteric portals for people who might have the same ability as I did; people who could help me match my previous experiences with my recognized abilities; people with whom I could exchange ideas.

At that time, Reiki was very trendy, and so I sought out a good Reiki teacher to initiate me in the technique. Within six months I had two initiations, and I became a Reiki master and teacher. Although I initially found the technique fascinating because I was controlling my energy for the first time, I ultimately didn't enjoy it. I noticed that something wasn't quite right with this method.

Certain symbols and terms are part of Reiki, and in strict schools a photograph of the founder of Reiki, Mikao Usui, who died in 1926, is displayed along with a candle. Yet I noticed that the room darkened as soon as the picture was put up; the same thing happened with the candle. When I worked with people, they felt warmth, but at the same time I felt that energy was being taken from me.

I got to know many Reiki masters, and remarkably, they all lived in (involuntary) financial poverty. This makes little sense, because if you have enough energy and are completely satisfied with your job, you can't be involuntarily financially poor. Someone will only lack money if they're suffering from a permanent loss of energy. Energy is also money – money is also energy. Reiki's many regulations and manipulations made the system impossible for me and my notion of personal freedom.

FINDING MY SPIRITUAL PATH

I was looking for a technique in which one doesn't lose energy and can remain a free person. I thought back to my teenage years: When I was 15, I met a naturopath who told me that I had very special energy and a special talent for working with people and helping them. She tried to give me an understanding of who I was and what made me tick. This therapist always had enough energy; she never seemed tired and, despite her mature years, looked extremely young.

Unfortunately, at the time when I was searching intensively for answers, she wasn't available to me. A 'stupid coincidence' or rightly so? At times like that I was at odds with my life, but something continued to drive me to find a solution.

So I continued searching for someone who could teach me how to use energy optimally, and that's how I came across a person who called himself the 'Sun Mage.' He invited me to Cancun in Mexico to show me his technique, and so I traveled there. The crazy thing was that the energy flowed out of his fingers like little pieces of fluff or lint. He touched people with it and helped them as a result.

This man didn't lose any energy in the process. He said he didn't have to teach me because I was able to do this from birth anyway. I stayed with him and watched him treat ministers, people from government, and high society in the city and across the country. He made a good living from his work and showed no signs of getting tired of it. I thought that, in him, I'd found someone who could understand me.

After four days in Cancun, I flew back to Frankfurt. Like the Sun Mage's other 'apprentices,' I was carrying a crystal ball from him in my luggage so that he could communicate with me and the others from afar. It took four weeks before my suspicions were confirmed that the man only wanted to make us dependent on him. Consequently, I backed away from him. I'm still convinced that people can be free; that as teachers we can give our students recommendations and tools, but that we have to let everyone develop freely.

My diverse inquiries taught me that many systems, consciously or unconsciously, ensure that people become dependent and make them susceptible to manipulation. I didn't want that under any circumstances! Many conversations with close friends and family confirmed to me that I should develop my own system, analyze my own experiences, write down what is useful – the essence of it – and make it accessible.

In my life I've now gone through various stages, and as a result I've been able to develop my talents and also act on my business skills. For many years I wanted to lay my 'special' abilities to rest and really only be successful in my business: I'd not only studied industrial engineering with a specialization in mechanical engineering, but also completed my studies in business administration.

After my studies, I wanted to do some proper business. Along the way, as had happened several times before, I'd ignored the fact that I had a talent and should use it wisely. That was probably how my life wanted it, and several people had already lovingly reminded me of it. But no, I opted for the shark tank again and was 'allowed' to experience rough times.

My sensitivity was a benefit to me in my professional life, and when I relied on myself, everything went perfectly. However, as soon as I tried to solve situations on a 'normal' intellectual basis – trying to behave like a bull on the New York Stock Exchange, or trying to understand people and business partners intellectually – what was desired often didn't occur.

This got me into trouble. I lost a lot of money and was humanly disappointed to the extreme several times. Afterward, I had to bounce back emotionally and financially. The positive side of this loss, however, was that I finally decided to banish intellectual decisions from my life and rely only on my intuition and the skills I'd had since birth. When I reminisce today, I can hardly believe that it would take so long for a person to recognize and feel out the good things in life.

A friend who worked with people energetically had long ago prophesied that I'd definitely have to take care of the energy work, or else suffer a setback and be forced to reorient myself. I ignored that as well, until I had a serious accident while skiing, tearing a bone in my knee. As I lay in the snow, I realized how it had happened: I'd been cursing all day because I'd had to queue for so long, and had constantly grumbled about how many people were on the slopes and the fact that I had no desire to ski among this hustle and bustle.

However, I was just as clear in my belief that I didn't want to be picked up either by helicopter or the rescue service. I decided to end the day of skiing 'as normal.' This definitive decision made any sensation of pain disappear and gave me control over my body. From today's perspective, I'd say that my affirmation of my situation was also 'acceptance' of it (a technique that now forms part of the MindFlow Method).

So I got up, and to avoid difficulties, I didn't put any weight on the broken leg. I practically went down the piste on one leg, and I eventually made it down into the valley in the gondola. I then had to be helped out of the gondola, but the worst part was the 15 steps I subsequently had to climb down. After that, I collapsed and was driven home in a car; I was later admitted to hospital for surgery.

When I woke up in the hospital bed after the operation, my knee hurt like hell – at first, it was almost unbearable. The pain dominated everything; it became a part of me. It turned out that the orthopedic device fitted during surgery had been incorrectly attached to my knee, and it was pressing directly onto the hole. Since I could neither get up nor remove the device, I only had óne option for the time being: to adopt complete 'acceptance' of the pain. And as a result, the pain was transformed into energy.

The surgeon told me that he'd really only seen accidents like this in children before. In his opinion, I would never properly run again and would certainly never be able to ski. What can I say? Six months later I was standing on skis again, and today I can kneel and move my knee without restrictions. (Tip: Anyone who has to do physical exercises, e.g. for the knee, can always exceed the pain threshold to a certain extent by 'accepting' the pain at the same time. However, guidance is needed for this!)

My knee was actually injured again in a fall in the French Alps near Courchevel, when I slid almost 1,000ft (300m) on bare ice into the valley. Wanting to appear cool, I'd jumped on my skis with youthful vigor, but slipped about 30ft (10m). That should have been warning enough for me, but no, my ego convinced me to attempt that youthful drive again. I wanted to show off and was reluctant to admit that I wasn't fit enough for such activities. I shot down toward the valley, tried to brake with my right leg, but twisted my knee and continued downhill. The fall only stopped when I accepted everything that was to come.

I wanted to get up calmly and signal to my friends up on the mountain that everything was okay. However, I immediately collapsed due to blows to my lungs. Back at the hotel, my right knee turned out to be completely swollen; everyone thought the vacation was over. I asked for 30 minutes to myself and withdrew. I used the MindFlow Method that we teach in the MindFlow basis seminar today, and after that, the knee was fine again. In the end, we were able to give our skiing vacation a happy ending. For me, however, it was clear by then that, at the very least, the ego severely hinders us, and as a result we only reach a kind of hubris that teaches us to stay grounded through a 'crash.'

USING MY GIFT IN BUSINESS

The friend who'd warned me to take care of the energy work had been pretty amused after my first knee injury and repeated her prediction after the second one. But as it is when you ultimately walk away from an accident without consequences, I again ignored the hint and kick-started my business career instead. I'd set up my own business consultancy specializing in mergers and acquisitions for companies in Germany, Austria, France, Switzerland, and the UK.

It went exceptionally well for years, until one evening in our kitchen I had a 'divine intervention' in the form of a serious heart attack. I felt the energy falling away, and it was as though my heart had stopped. I couldn't breathe – it was as if I'd been switched off. Then I collapsed.

That scared me. I'd always had enough energy, and I felt invincible all the time, despite many difficult experiences. I'd survived so many cuts in my life, and suddenly I was weak. It was as if life wanted to say to me: *Either you take on the tasks that are intended for you now, or you leave!* At least that's what I felt. That must have been when I finally decided wholeheartedly on my vocation.

At the moment of my decision I was already certain that my heart was regenerating. The constriction opened, and it grew warm. The mitochondria, and at the same time my entire system, likely ramped up their activity. About five minutes after I had this breakdown, I got up, recovered, and was like new overnight. I remembered the vocation that I'd brought with me to this Earth. To be on the safe side, I nevertheless consulted a doctor the next day for investigations. All fine, he said.

But the warning had been clear enough – and it was the starting gun for my public energetic work. I'd taken the hint: I could either pass on my knowledge or no longer be needed! I decided to work in my company for three days a week and work energetically with people two days a week.

When people seeking advice came to me, I asked only for their name beforehand, no other information. I described their issues and situations to them without having a conversation with them first. I always say that anyone can master a so-called 'cold reading'! As an example, a businesswoman consulted me because she wanted to move in with her life partner. Without intending to be disrespectful, I made her understand that in my mind's eye, I saw a woman at her side, not a man; she then burst into tears and told me that she'd harbored a secret lesbian love for a long time.

Another client asked me if he should cancel a business order for almost 5 million euros. He had concerns about the customer in question, who was very different from himself, but at the same time he was afraid of missing out on a hefty profit and being unable to reward his employees. My prediction was that there would definitely be another, far better, opportunity and the company would experience a change in strategy as a result.

So my client canceled his order in a very honest letter, and within a week he'd gained a new customer. His company created a very special portfolio with the new customer that perfectly matched its structures and skills, and today it's recommended for these kinds of specialized tasks.

The more I was lucky enough to guide people and teach them how to use energy, the clearer it became to me that everyone works in the same way. It's always about the level of energy: When it's high, people are healthy; if it's low, people suffer from poor health. So I devoted myself intensively to the testing and development of techniques with which each individual can raise his or her energy level and thereby regenerate the body.

I passed the selection process for training with various masters and teachers who have millennia-old oral knowledge in the areas of healing, resilience, and independence – knowledge that was reserved for only a few. Gradually my MindFlow Method crystallized, a technique that I'm finally making available to the general public. I think the time is ripe to pass on the knowledge to others rather than keep it hidden.

In my professional career, I had to deal with plenty of difficult people: Men and women with big egos who had manipulated others and pushed them into the abyss. I'm now clearly aware that in my original job, and in my company, I wasn't able to offer as much positive help as I'm able to do today with MindFlow.

My wish is to use these techniques to show people that everyone can be free and shape their own future if they have enough energy; nobody should be abused and manipulated by others. The side effect of a lot of energy is a life that's filled with happiness, joy, and prosperity.

WHAT TO EXPECT
FROM THIS BOOK

Every person is different and perceives things in their own way. Consequently, each of us has our own version of reality. Quite often we limit ourselves in what we *are*, and instead try to achieve what we *want* to be. This *wanting* tends to come from an external source, stimulated as a desire within us by advertising, family, or society.

A huge problem lies in wanting things, and reaching a goal by wanting requires a great deal of energy. Every goal that I define for myself signals to my character that I must be something or achieve something. But in that moment, I lack the very thing that I'd like to achieve or which I long for. As a result, I focus on this insufficiency and need an enormous amount of energy to contain it.

This 'lack mindset,' in combination with techniques that work on wanting, such as setting and achieving goals, causes a significant loss of energy. And in addition, someone who has set a goal has already fundamentally limited themselves!

In thermodynamics, the universal law of the conservation of energy states: 'In a closed system the sum of all energy is constant; the total energy is conserved over time.' Therefore, if I have too little energy, I must have given it up at some point in the past. The German physicist Hermann von Helmholtz (1821–1894) expressed it in even more detail: 'Energy can be neither generated nor destroyed. It can only be converted from one form into another form, or be transmitted from one body to another body.'

'Blocks' are an accumulation of energy, and people who have the relevant knowledge and techniques can utilize this energy for the benefit of themselves and others. This book presents some of these techniques to a wider audience. MindFlow is based on ancient knowledge that for thousands of years has only been passed down orally from masters to their students. As a master of this ancient system, I've processed this knowledge and have converted it into the MindFlow Method in order to make it accessible to many people.

Do you think that you have too much energy? Then please, put this book aside or give it away. If, on the other hand, you feel as if you don't have enough energy, then I say to you: 'Welcome!' At its core, the MindFlow Method leads to an increase in the energy level of our bodies. In this way, it's possible for us to assume a heightened state of consciousness that we call 'G4.'

This book will allow you to get to know the techniques that can help you gain additional energy. I'll begin by letting you in on a secret: When you have enough energy, all of your conflicts and problems will resolve themselves by what we call 'Not-Doing'!

Yours,

Tom Moegele

HOW MINDFLOW WILL
CHANGE YOUR LIFE

Most of us aim to avoid stress, anger, and conflict. This is completely understandable because stress *blocks* the flow of life energy and our energy level drops; however, the consequences of these blocks and drops in energy include illness, exhaustion, psychological disorders, and, in the most general sense, a weakening of body and soul.

The good news is that you can take advantage of the stress you face when, for example, someone is furious with you. Instead of dismissing the stress as something negative, you can simply see it as a form of energy that's available to you. Let's say your boss is taking out their moods on you. Super! Instead of letting them break your nerves and steal your energy in the process, you can use the tools and practices presented in this book to ensure that they don't succeed in getting you down; on the contrary, you can raise your own energy level with this concentrated form of energy.

It's a win-win situation – the boss also benefits as they'll cast off some of their own blocks, and their energy level will also increase. To accomplish this, you'll need to switch to what we call the 'G4 consciousness,' and the following chapters will describe how this works. But first, I'd like to give you an idea of how, when you're in G4, you can trigger another person's block in everyday life 'as if by chance' and contribute to its resolution.

When I fly I often wear a very casual outfit, and on a recent trip to Berlin, despite traveling business class, I was dressed in shorts, a T-shirt with holes, and running shoes. As I was standing on the boarding bridge, a man in a suit pushed past me, almost rolling his suitcase over my foot. *Wow, so much energy!* I thought. I made space for him and extended an inviting gesture: 'You're welcome to fly *ahead* of me.' He looked at me – beat-up as I was – and his jaw dropped.

Now, to make matters worse, he faced the big problem of sitting in the same row as me. I had the aisle seat in row 3, while he sat in the window seat. I turned to him and said: 'Oh, so we're flying together after all!' After sitting down the man quickly opened his laptop and started tapping away. He didn't drink anything during the flight, nor eat breakfast. As we were disembarking, I took another step back in the aisle to make room for him and said: 'Well, well, you're in a hurry. Go ahead!' I didn't treat him badly and I didn't call him names. I just indicated: 'Hey, it's okay, it's cool...' *I had energy.*

The next time that man is on the boarding bridge do you think he'll shove past another passenger and roll his suitcase over their feet? No, most likely not. *That's* the healing! Even if it seemed for a moment as if the man was standing there like a loser, in reality he'd just lost his *block*! He'd lost the *need* to push in front.

The man could just as easily have laughed at my remark – that would have been the 'right' response. Then we'd have spoken for a while, and everything would have been fine. Equally, I could have gone into fight mode and laid claim to my space with a corresponding announcement. But with my unruffled reaction, I thoroughly enjoyed the flight. I kept looking over at the man and thinking: *The poor guy is having to pound away at his laptop now.*

With MindFlow, we no longer need to fight with others – instead, we can interact with them!

USING THE BOOK

This book is designed for people who find themselves in strained situations: those who are experiencing problems with their family, their partner, their children, or in their job. Once you've read this book and integrated MindFlow into your life, things will become easier. In my seminars I always say, provocatively: 'Life will then become boring.' Why? Because you'll be free of stress and will learn to realign your life on a higher level.

However, this book isn't merely about grasping the MindFlow Method on an intellectual level; in addition, you'll find body and energy exercises that'll enable you to understand it on an even deeper level. This knowledge will pass into the consciousness of your cells. *Yes*, our cells have consciousness and possess their own intelligence. Once they've experienced something positive, they'll want to repeat this experience.

When we're in G4, which is an elevated state of consciousness, the release of two hormones intensifies: Serotonin, the happiness hormone, and the bonding hormone oxytocin, which has the 'side effect' of making us look younger as it relaxes our muscles.

My advice is to read this book several times:

- **Part I, Introducing MindFlow,** contains the knowledge required to be able to understand MindFlow on an intellectual level and to get to grips with the individual principles.

- **Part II, MindFlow in Practice,** contains exercises you can use to enter G4. You'll also learn how to use the energies of other people and situations to your advantage, without harming anyone.

In some chapters, topics are touched on only briefly, before being explained in greater detail later in the book. So if there are concepts, mindsets, or exercises that you don't instantly understand, just read on. Each piece of knowledge builds up on top of the others, eventually generating a full picture. In Chapter 12, a power tool awaits you, which you can use to change your life quickly and in a sustained, positive way.

A Testimonial

Before we begin, I'd like to give you another example of how MindFlow works and takes effect, so that you can more easily integrate the theoretical background information presented in the coming chapters.

A participant in one of my seminars explained that dogs often barked at her in the street and sometimes even attacked her. She had a 'block' because as a child she'd been bitten by a Border collie that she'd wanted to stroke. Since then she'd harbored an extreme phobia of dogs, which she inevitably communicated to the animals. Even tame and gentle dogs went after her.

After working with the MindFlow Method for just one weekend, the woman was able to resolve the block. Today, she likes dogs, and even has a small dog herself, a true companion who goes everywhere with her. She's also able to walk the streets again without fear. Dogs now react peacefully toward her, and some even express a desire to be stroked. From this example, we can recognize that the resolution of a block can have a very strong impact on our life.

The chapter that follows explores the science that underpins the MindFlow Method. If it's too dry for you, you can skip over the first part and just read the section headed 'Burkhard Heim's Unified Quantum Field Theory,' which contains information important to an understanding of our forthcoming work with energy and the G4 consciousness.

PART I

INTRODUCING
MINDFLOW

Chapter 1

QUANTA, DIMENSIONS, AND THE LIGHT OF LIFE

In this chapter, I've outlined the basic principles of the physics behind the MindFlow Method in extremely simplified terms – without the use of mathematical equations and formulas that are almost impossible for the layperson to understand. My hope is that this basic knowledge will ensure that the information in subsequent chapters is easy to comprehend.

The tools and exercises featured in this book have been developed and compiled on the basis of my own experiences. There are also quantum-physical models (more on these later) that explain what I experience in my own work – those that mystics and healers have passed down as spiritual knowledge and secret lore for millennia.

THE ZERO-POINT FIELD

Physicists, from Galileo Galilei to Albert Einstein and Werner Heisenberg, have described the laws that underlie the experiential world. They were trying to explain something that can't really be understood by humans 'trapped' in the three-dimensional world of the body, as quantum physics is beyond our sense of 'reason.'

The famous US quantum physicist Richard Feynman coined the saying: 'If you think you understand quantum physics, you don't understand quantum physics.' Although quantum physics provides reliable formulas for calculating the probability of subatomic states, it also illustrates that there are applicable laws that defy human perception, or even contradict it. For example, it's impossible to precisely determine both location and speed simultaneously. Einstein, in turn, is credited with saying: 'I would like to spend the rest of my life reflecting on what light is.' As we'll see in this chapter, he got to the heart of the matter.

According to the considerations and deductions of quantum physics, the entire cosmos can be reduced to a fundamental, primal energy: the so-called 'zero-point field' or 'quantum field.' In the world's ancient mystic and spiritual traditions, too, this field was thought of as the source of all creation and all beings; in fact, we could also call it 'God' or the 'spirit.'

PHOTONS

In the branch of science called particle physics, photons (subatomic particles) are known as carriers or particles of light, or as the quanta (bundles of energy) of the electromagnetic field. Less well known are the so-called biophotons or light quanta. Biophysics draws a direct link between vitality/ quality of life/consciousness and the quantity and quality of light quanta, which affect the entire organism and regulate all vital processes in our energy field. A constant exchange of information about these light quanta takes place on the cellular level of the human organism.

Research into biophotons was advanced by the German biophysicist Fritz-Albert Popp, among others; he, in turn, drew upon the findings of Russian doctors related to the biological exchange of information from cells via photons in the ultraviolet range. Taken together, Popp's findings can be broken down to show that this communication cannot be based on biochemical processes alone, given that this type of signal transmission is too slow. Rather, the biophoton field represents the highest level of biological control functions. Accordingly, the electromagnetic field that surrounds our physical bodies is by no means merely a meaningless 'waste product' of the chemical processes that occur in the body. In fact, it plays the leading role, as it were – regulating all vital processes in the organism. With this in mind, the concept of biophotons – the 'light of life' as coined by Popp – should be understood quite literally.

In the context of modern physics, the biophoton field – an intangible carrier field through which measurable biophoton signals travel – is equivalent to a purely electromagnetic body of energy. Further subtle dimensions, known in the esoteric tradition as light bodies or etheric bodies, are excluded from this context.

As a part of the cosmos, the human is, ultimately, energy – both the physical body and the thoughts and the soul. In turn, body, mind, and spirit exert permanent influence on one another; the importance of this mutual exchange is increasingly being recognized by corresponding research in the field of psychosomatic medicine. Simple techniques empower us to make contact with the source of all energy – the quantum field – and to make use of this energy.

BURKHARD HEIM'S UNIFIED QUANTUM FIELD THEORY

One of the greatest and most controversial scientists of our time was the German theoretical physicist Burkhard Heim (1925–2001). In formulating his unified quantum field theory, he took four physical laws set out by nature as a starting point:

1. The first law of thermodynamics, or the law of the conservation of energy. This states that, in a closed system, energy can neither be lost nor gained.

2. The second law of thermodynamics, or the law of entropy (entropy is the measure of disorder in a system). The law of entropy states that the entire universe tends toward chaos. A disordered, disorganized state is only reversible in the event of corresponding external energy input.

3. The law of quantization, or Planck's radiation law. According to this, everything can be broken down to the smallest discrete and measurable bundles of energy – the quanta.

4. The law of the existence of macroscopic (far-reaching) fields: a) gravitational field; b) electromagnetic field (photon field).

Heim's Model of the Universe

Heim worked with the so-called 'Minkowski Space,' named after the German mathematician Hermann Minkowski (1864–1909), who, in 1907, posited a four-dimensional vector space with which Albert Einstein's 1905 special theory of relativity can be formulated very elegantly, and which also forms the basis of Einstein's 1916 theory of general relativity.

Simply put, space (three-dimensionality) and time (the fourth dimension) are brought together here in a unified, four-dimensional structure known as 'spacetime.' On the basis of this, Heim developed a model of the cosmos with 12 dimensions:

- The tangible physical dimensions X1–X3: space (length, width, height)

- The temporal (time) dimension X4

- The etheric organizational dimensions X5 (structure) and X6 (time)

- The informational dimensions X7 and X8

- The spiritual dimensions, or the spiritual 'hyperspace' (higher dimension) of G4 (X9–X12)

For our purposes, we'll call these dimensions D1–D12. Heim's equations provided him with four distinct groups of elementary particles, which he called 'last units':

1. Electrically charged particles with six coordinates (D1–D6)

2. Neutral particles with the coordinates D1, D2, D3, D5, and D6 (so without the time dimension D4)

3. So-called intermediate particles (bosons) with the coordinates D4, D5, and D6

4. Quanta of the gravitational field (gravitons, activities) with the coordinates D5 and D6

According to Heim's model, 'access' to the world of matter is always possible from the spiritual hyperspace of G4, and indeed from D7 and D8, the informational dimensions, and from the organizational space of D5 and D6. Computer-aided checks of Heim's theories prove that they match the corresponding measurements down to the last decimal.

Ultimately, Heim's model states that the cosmos developed in a first step from G4 – the spiritual 'archetypes' – and that matter developed in a second step. The term 'LOGOS' was coined to describe these spiritual archetypes in the traditions of ancient wisdom, and in the Bible it was incorrectly translated as 'word': The 'word' made flesh is a metaphor for the descent of the spirit (G4) from energy (D5–D8) into matter.

Heim says that all 'last units' contain the 'trans-dimensions' D5 and D6. Thereby, the 5th dimension as the measure of organization is inverse to the concept of entropy, the measure of disorganization, and the 6th dimension controls this organization in time. You could express it like this: D5 represents all possible structures in the cosmos and D6 represents their realization in time in D4. Heim differentiated between latent events – those taking place 'in the background' – in the trans-space of D5 and D6 as possible causes for the manifest events in Einstein's R4, i.e. in dimensions D1–D4.

THE 12 DIMENSIONS: D1-D12

So, to recap, according to Heim's dimensional laws, there are 12 dimensions. D1–D3 are interchangeable (length, width, height), whereas all of the others are not. D7 and D8 are, like D5 and D6, informational dimensions that can create and destroy energy in the short term.

Heim divided the 12 dimensions into a reference space, D1–D6, and a hyperspace, D7–D12. As you can see in the table below, dimensions D1–D3 belong to the physical, material reality; these stand for the tangible world. D4 represents time. All the other dimensions describe energetic or spiritual spaces: D5 and D6 are organizational, and D7 and D8 are informational spaces. D9–D12 form what's known as the 'hyperspace' (higher dimension) of the spirit, which in the course of our work, we'll call G4.

D1	D2	D3			R3	Physical space (three-dimensionality)
D4					T	Time
D1	D2	D3	D4		R4	Spacetime
D5	D6				S2	Organizational space
D7	D8				I2	Informational space
D9	D10	D11	D12		G4	Hyperspace

The 12 dimensions
by reference space and hyperspace

We'll leave it there for now. We need this basic information for the following chapter, but don't worry – you don't need to have a physics degree to apply these pearls of wisdom.

So, in summary, we can say that:

- Matter, for the most part, is made up of fields. These fields are held together by quanta without proper mass – mainly virtual photons – which determine the structure of the matter, and so are superordinate to matter. In physics, they're known as 'intermediate quanta.'

- The most important intermediate quanta are the quanta of the electromagnetic field, including visible light, today generally known as 'photons.'

- In the cosmos as well as in the human body, there are almost 1 billion times more biophotons than material particles. Therefore, the cosmos consists primarily of *light*.

- Of the 12 dimensions, D1–D3 belong to the physical, three-dimensional reality; D4 represents time. The other dimensions are energetic or spiritual spaces: D5 and D6 are organizational; D7 and D8 are informational; D9–D12 are the 'hyperspace' of the spirit, or G4.

- Everything is controlled by G4, which was characterized in the traditions of old as 'God,' the 'world spirit,' 'original source,' or similar. We'll be delving further into G4 in the following chapters.

Heim's theory can be used to explain many real-world phenomena. My personal experiences with the 12 dimensions and G4 consciousness – that is, the spiritual dimensions D9–D12 – can also be explained with reference to Heim's findings as a theoretical base. Interestingly, the so-called Jacob's Ladder (staircase) is described in Genesis 28:12 in the Bible as having 12 rungs, the number corresponding to the numbering of the verses: 12! In the analogy, Jesus in the New Testament is considered the new ladder to Heaven (John 1:51), and he had 12 disciples.

Heim tried to describe the world with his 12 dimensions. As soon as we work with energy, we proceed to a 'divine' level from which we're able to control the world.

A Trip Through the 12 Dimensions

For us humans, all 'perceptible' events *appear* to take place in Einstein's spacetime, R4 (D1–D4). However, this is not the case, and in order to show you this, we'll take a journey through the dimensions together.

The physical space D1–D3 corresponds to the tangible, terrestrial world, with its three (geometrical) dimensions of length, width, and height. The fourth dimension, D4, is time, or Einstein's spacetime. It continues with the etheric structural spaces D5 and D6 – the energetic control dimensions – which intervene in an organizational manner in the physical D1–D4 area of matter. D7 and D8 are the

	Burkhard Heim	Esoteric/spiritual teachings
D12	G4 consciousness	Spiritual level
D11		
D10		
D9		
D8	Global information field I2	2nd causal level
D7	Global information field I1	1st causal level
D6	Energetic control field S2	Mental level
D5	Energetic control field S1	Astral level
D4	Time	Time
D3	z coordinates	Height
D2	y coordinates	Width
D1	x coordinates	Length

Heim's 12-dimensional world

informational dimensions; individual as well as collective information patterns are found here. The dimensions D9–D12 represent the hyperspace, or the spiritual dimension of G4.

Here are a few examples of the way the dimensions work:

- If someone thinks they're seeing spirits or astral beings, which dimension are they in? D5.

- When we're doing mental programming and emotional work, we're in D6.

- When a person is permanently pushed for time, they're in D4.

ENERGY BLOCKS AND LIFE ENERGY

A human being is an energetic vortex: Energy, which carries within it the 'divine spark,' flows around us. Every person has a specific amount of life energy available. However, we all carry within us energy *blocks* that impede the flow of our life energy. As one of these blocks is released, life energy is set free.

There are many approaches for using this life energy for healing and liberation: for example, acupuncture, massage, or relaxation techniques. In our work we take ourselves into the space of G4. We do so not only to dismantle blocks, but also to transform them into energy that's of benefit to ourselves and to those with whom we interact. We dismantle blocks by Not-Doing or Not-Wanting: that is, *without* the use of goal-oriented behavior. You'll learn about this in Chapter 6, 'The Concept of Not-Doing.'

The law of the conservation of energy states that the total amount of energy in a system always remains the same. However, this law no longer applies in G4; otherwise, mathematically speaking, matter would run against infinity. This is what makes our approach unique. Only in G4 can one change something on a spiritual level without doing anything, and without potentially losing energy through interacting with another person. This can be used in healing work, for example, but also in everyday contact with other people.

TESTIMONIAL
Daniel from Switzerland

In 2009 I experienced a period of burnout that lasted for several weeks. Shortly after, my family fell apart, and I really hit rock bottom.

Since I've got to know Tom's work, though, everything has changed. The knowledge that he communicates is very easy to apply. I get up in the morning and have so much strength and power; I have the feeling that I could tear down trees! And by the evening I'm still feeling fit. As a result of performing the asanas, as well as my frequent presence in G4, I retain my strength and energy through the day.

This is the beauty of this simple exercise. You can feel it the very first time you use it: You do it and you think, *Wow, that helps.* All of the other techniques and methods I'd tried in the past just didn't have this effect.

I lead a company with 25 employees in central Switzerland, and before I got to know Tom in 2013, I wasn't far off another period of burnout. Yet since I've integrated the concept of MindFlow into my life and the company, I've transformed my entire environment. The company's doing better and I'm doing better. It's an absolute win-win situation. Just brilliant. Since I've been doing this work to stay with myself, I find that conflicts no longer pose a challenge. Instead, they become just a game that I play. I know how to play it and the conflicts resolve themselves very easily. And as a consequence of this, I *love* conflicts!

Chapter 2

ENERGY - THE BASICS

In this chapter we'll look at the fundamental principles of energy to help you understand how to work with it in the right way.

THE NADIS

The Sanskrit word 'nadi' essentially means 'pipe,' 'channel,' or 'flow,' and it describes the subtle energy channels in the body through which the energy of life, the prana, flows. The nadis are more delicate than the neural pathways of the brain and are closely connected with the nervous system. They're supplied with energy via the chakras – the body's energy centers. Nadis are found all over the body.

Through using the Mindflow Method, you'll learn to release your energy blocks, and once this takes place, the stored energy will flow back into the nadis and circulate in your whole body system.

The three most important nadis are the Sushumna, Ida, and Pingala. As in the symbol of the Caduceus (*see below*), the Ida and Pingala nadis follow a spiral pattern around the Sushumna nadi, in which the 'kundalini' energy is led from the bottom to the top. The Caduceus is a symbolic representation of the 'awakened' human – what's meant here by then kundalini energy which then radiates over the crown chakra to the right and left.

The Caduceus

Sushumna Nadi

The word 'Sushumna' means 'penetrating current.' The Sushumna nadi represents Sattva, the rhythm beyond duality. It's the central channel connecting the root chakra with the crown chakra – or Earth with Heaven. The kundalini is awakened via the Sushumna nadi by breathing through both nostrils.

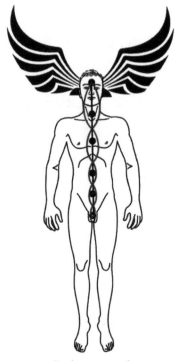

Sushumna nadi

Ida Nadi

In Sanskrit, 'Ida' means 'comfort.' This energy channel begins to the left of the Sushumna nadi, in the left testicle in men and the left ovary in women, and ends at the left nostril. The Ida nadi stands for feminine energy, representing both introverted characteristics and the left side of the body, and is connected to the right side of the brain; it has a cooling effect on the body. It's also associated with lunar energy, and it has control over all mental processes.

Pingala Nadi

The word 'Pingala' also comes from Sanskrit and means 'tawny' or 'orange.' This energy channel begins to the right of the Sushumna channel, in the right testicle in men and the right ovary in women, and ends at the right nostril.

The Pingala nadi embodies masculine energy and, in contrast to Ida, it raises the temperature of the body. Pingala is represented by the right side of the body and the left side of the brain. It correlates with Surya, the sun, and is associated with solar energy; this nadi is particularly active during solar storms. Pingala controls all of the body's vital functions and outwardly represents extroverted characteristics.

THE LAYERS OF THE AURA AND HEALING

Each of us has an aura – an energy field that surrounds the physical body – with at least seven layers. The seventh layer, which is the uppermost, can sometimes even be palpable at a distance of 0.5–1 mile (1–2km). Issues and emotional blocks travel across the layers of the aura from the outside to the inside. From the second layer of the aura, diseases begin to make themselves known; in the first layer, they manifest in the body.

The G4 consciousness works in all seven layers of the aura, because as a spiritual hyperspace it can influence all levels.

IMPLANTS

In our MindFlow work, 'implants' are energetic patterns that are set externally, and which exert a sustained influence on people. In children, implants are often placed by parents, teachers, or other adults; in this way, these individuals hand down their patterns and experiences of 'how life works.' This often occurs without ill intent – it tends to be an unconscious process.

And therein lies the problem. There are numerous implants that block the free flow of energy and make acceptance within the G4 consciousness difficult. For example, there are people who believe that they're only worthy of being loved when they behave 'appropriately,' or those who limit themselves and are able only to accept the love of others under certain conditions or to a limited degree.

ENERGY BLOCKS AND MINDFLOW

As we discussed in the previous chapter, a block compresses the flow of energy, preventing it from moving freely and unhindered. This shows up in all kinds of possible symptoms and complaints from anxiety to divorce, and in the form of diseases on a physical level. A block can form as a result of implants or traumatic experiences, but also as a result of thought patterns and belief systems that one has become accustomed to over the years.

The MindFlow Method is about handing back responsibility to individuals. By increasing energy, MindFlow places the body in a state in which it can resolve the blocks itself, and in which the free and natural flow of energy can be restored. Consequently, this technique can help with health problems as well as in areas related to relationships, finances, and emotions.

THE ENERGY SYSTEM

Put very simply, the human system can be divided into the following entities:

- The intellect

- The subconscious, including the nervous system

- The higher self/God level/the Creator

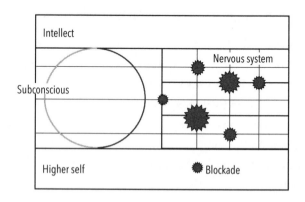

The energy system

In the previous illustration, the intellect is located above the nervous system; the higher self is beneath the nervous system; and the subconscious sits alongside the nervous system. The circle represents life. Something must emerge (the left/lighter half of the circle) and something must die away (the right/darker half of the circle). People prefer the emergence to the dying away. However, a farmer who has harvested apples from the tree in autumn doesn't cry – they know that there'll be apples again next year. The same is true of life energy – everything appears, and then disappears. The cycle of life is complete; it functions, regardless of whether we believe in it or not.

The higher self generates tasks for us that are stored in the nervous system in the form of blocks – some of which we've generated ourselves; some we've carried with us from birth; and others we've received from our surroundings. A block acts like a road sign. For example, we get back pain because we've worked ourselves too hard, and if we look at the sign saying 'Back Pain,' we can address it. However, if instead we take a painkiller, the reasons for the back pain can't be worked through. The higher self looks and says: *Has the block gone? No? Okay, then I'll put something else on it.* This continues until we resolve the block.

The problem with this is that we can't overcome this block in the area of the mind that lies 'above.' What happens on the intellectual level has no direct access to the nervous system and cannot resolve blocks in the nervous system.

As humans we preserve experiences. The body has an incorruptible memory, the physical memory. I won't forget anything I've experienced with my body: the body can recall the memory at any time. The solar plexus 'remembers' everything – like an elephant – with radiations in the direction of the throat chakra and the sacral chakra. If the solar plexus has been offended often, there's a tendency for neck or thyroid problems to develop; this is often seen in women who aren't allowed to speak their minds.

All the emotions that we experience reside in energy stores that build up over the years. For example, when we feel empathy for someone, a vortex begins, and we are carried along by its momentum. However, this isn't necessary; it only intensifies the emotions instead of resolving them. We want to use the energy rather than preserve it in storage. When we react to certain people in a certain way, it's like the light being turned on in an energy store – the block becomes visible.

For example, if I say: 'On principle, I don't like any man with a beard,' that's due to a block. Unconsciously, I then seek out men with beards in order to resolve the block. The same applies if somebody chooses similar-looking wives or husbands over the course of five marriages – the issue isn't resolved. As soon as the person affected resolves the issue, they're free. They don't even have to end a relationship; they can continue with it, but without the entanglement.

As issues or emotions are resolved with the help of what we call the 'energy acceptance technique,' energy is contained in storage, or the 'water tank,' and can be used (you'll learn about these concepts in Chapter 10, 'The Energy Acceptance Technique'). The emotions themselves and the manner in which they're resolved shouldn't be judged. One person might start to gasp, another to twitch, while yet another might shout or cry – but they're letting out the emotions without judgment or getting involved with them. The emotions will simply dissolve; there's no reason to hold on to emotions.

With MindFlow, we're 'anchoring' nothing – instead we're entering G4 – and in this moment, nothing is static anymore. None of these emotions exist; everything is merely a hormonal reaction in the body. As soon as the emotions are gone, the 'water tank' dries up and isn't refilled. Once a block is resolved, energy can flow from G4. Many of my clients and seminar participants then report a short period of conflict; an energy reservoir has been tapped and the energy within suddenly starts to flow. Old disputes dissolve as if into thin air, and relationships and situations take on completely new directions.

In the testimonials that appear in certain chapters, you'll see what can change in life once a block has been resolved. In the course of the book, we'll focus on how you can bring your own energy and the energy of those around you back into flow. This is how blocks can be resolved. However, to really release deep-seated blocks and, above all, implants,

I recommend you consult one of the MindFlow experts trained by me; visit www.mindflow.academy to find a list of experts organized by zip code.

THE MITOCHONDRIA – POWER STATIONS OF THE CELLS

Mitochondria are minuscule filament-like cell organelles that convert carbohydrates into energy through their metabolism. They form their own unit in the cell; it's thought that they developed in the cell at some point during the course of evolution. The mitochondria live in symbiosis with the cells and deliver energy to them, which is why they're known as the 'power stations of the cells.'

There are similar cases in nature, so a visual comparison is possible. There are, for example, jellyfish that harbor algae. The algae carry out photosynthesis and the jellyfish are able to harness the resulting energy.

The mitochondria produce fuel for the cells: adenosine triphosphate (ATP). In order to produce ATP, the mitochondria burn oxygen. We breathe in oxygen, which reaches the body's cells via the blood, and there the mitochondria get to work, converting the energy from our food into ATP. Every cell is at risk if the mitochondria are damaged; then the cells are no longer completely able to fulfill their purpose – which has an effect on the cell structure, the organs, and even the body in its entirety. Diseases develop.

The mitochondria also control the process of apoptosis (cell death) as well as the frequency and speed of cell division. The activity of the mitochondria also influences the pineal gland, which regulates many processes in the body. With powerful, fit mitochondria, a person is healthy and lives life with strength. With weak mitochondria, our systems no longer function properly.

When you enter G4, the mitochondria ramp up their activity within seconds; this is measurable through the increased emission of body heat. Using a thermal imaging camera or brain frequency imaging, we can observe how the mitochondria react to interactions with other humans or in a particular context; for example, the boss who verbally attacks an employee is potentially giving off less energy than her employee. If the employee reacts to the criticism, his mitochondria 'power down' their activity while the boss's mitochondria 'ramp up' theirs.

As long as the mitochondria are in a good condition, they'll send the cells into programmed cell death: As a cell nears death, the mitochondria fire – to put it simply – a 'hand grenade' into the cell so that the old cell can destroy itself and be fed into the system. The body eats its cells (which are mainly protein) and uses them up.

If the mitochondria aren't working properly, they'll pull the safety pin – to take the metaphor further – on the hand grenade, but aren't actually able to set it off. The hand grenade's safety catch has been released, but the cells are not able to die. Now the cells are changing, degenerating, and illness looms. In the worst cases, cancer can develop. The level of energy is low.

What happens to most people when they're sick? They're treated by a doctor, which means the illness is given significance as it's being paid attention. Instead, we could accept the illness and simply observe it. The illness is allowed to be. Consequently, the illness loses energy – something that the affected person is currently lacking. When the body has more energy available again, it's able to recover. Every disease develops, correspondingly, due to a lack of energy or weak mitochondria. A person with strong mitochondria will not become sick.

The day after a MindFlow seminar, many of the participants feel completely shattered. It's important to know this, and again, I'll explain it with a metaphor. The glass filled with liquid is clear at first – sediment has settled at the bottom. However, if the liquid is set in motion and energy is brought back into the system, everything is stirred up.

This is what happens if we translate this image: The mitochondria boot up, and at this moment, they effectively set off the 'hand grenade.' This means that many cells that should have long since died do so and are disposed of. This is why it's three to five days after a seminar or a MindFlow session before participants return to a normal level again: Energy is ramped up, and a lot of 'garbage' is sluiced out of the body. In medicine this is called the 'initial aggravation.'

With more energy in the body, cognition is also improved due to more active mitochondria and comprehension becomes more complex. More energy = improved perception! The person isn't just less vulnerable to attack, they also notice more. With more energy, a person can also absorb more attacks.

And all of this is 'only' because we entered G4 and 'did nothing' there (you'll learn all about this Chapter 6, 'The Concept of Not-Doing').

TESTIMONIAL
Soultana from Munich, Germany

This is the case of a 56-year-old patient who had been made redundant from her long-term employment six months earlier and was extremely irritated and distressed because she had no idea how she'd find another job. She came to my practice to deal with other issues and mentioned this incident in passing.

I treated her, and afterward she returned to me, beaming with joy and saying that she'd found a position through the job center and was very happy. The new job paid more money that the last one, the conditions were markedly better, and the new boss had been determined to get her specifically to take on this role. She could hardly believe it: after all, she was 'just' an unskilled worker, and not a young one at that. As people work on themselves and resolve their blocks, life unfolds for them and constructive solutions appear. And for that, I'm very grateful.

In my practice, I also find working with children and young people very satisfying. Their parents bring them to me because they're under enormous pressure at school and are exhibiting very pronounced symptoms of stress. Among the children I treat, the change is noticeable after the first session. By the second session, the children arrive with much more relaxed expressions and tell me that schooling is already much more fun and that they no longer have to learn quite so much, in the sense of 'cramming.' Their relationship with their parents and other students also improves. They report that they like going to school a lot more, and even look forward to it. And, of course, that makes me even happier because I've done nothing but work with them using the MindFlow Method. The changes are lasting.

Chapter 3

THE ENERGY LEVELS

Every one of us emits a 'standing wave,' which is individually produced by our DNA, and can be disrupted if we have particular issues or blocks. It's possible to read the standing wave – it's even possible to recognize people from their standing wave, even when blindfolded. Every human is permanently and unconsciously reading the waves of others, and unfortunately this means that we judge people with our minds.

The standing wave

Some people can read standing waves in order to obtain information, as if they were Morse code signals. When someone comes to my practice, I initially want no verbal information from them. Why? Well, the client wants a solution to a problem, and if I started talking to them straight away, I'd be able to figure out everything in a so-called 'cold reading' – just as anyone could. The art is in telling the client their issues without the client having spoken about them. They then realize that they're obviously giving away these issues on the outside – because issues present as a standing wave.

Every one of us also has a personal energy field, which can be measured. There's a constant transfer of energy between people in a room. The energy always travels from those with more energy to those who have less energy.

But we know a state – G4 – in which you'll not *concede* any energy; instead you'll only *absorb* energy, and as a result, you can help others to resolve their blocks. In G4 you receive energy and are no longer vulnerable.

To ease your first steps into this chapter, I'll give you a few examples using numbers:

- A 'normal human' has 50–60% life energy.

- A person with less than 50% life energy is entering the zone of illness; the lower the life energy, the sicker the person.

- At 50% life energy a person will also have 50% in the form of energy blocks. At 80% life energy, there will be 20% in energy blocks.

ENERGY LEVELS IN D1–D3

Most people have energy-related blocks on the dimensions D1–D3; as a result they can reach a maximum personal life energy level of 40%. They've almost lost the full connection to their divinity and are struggling for survival, not just in daily life but also in the energetic sense. With an energy level of 40%, no personal development can take place at all. This is why something outside of R4 (spacetime, according to Einstein) intervenes to force a development. The everyday life of these people is characterized by illness, poverty, worry, misery, and anger; and they use their anger to draw energy away from people with a higher level of energy.

The next illustration (*see page 66*) is based on the law of the conservation of energy, which remains valid within the dimensions D1–D3. The person on the left, who was originally at an energy level of 40%, *lost* 10% of his energy (Δ) through interacting with the person on the right, whose energy level was originally at 20%; and the person on the right *received* 10% of energy (Δ). So the total energy of the closed system of 60% therefore remains constant ($\sum$).

Energy levels in D1-D3

	40%	20%
Δ	-10%	+10%
Σ	30%	30%

This can also be illustrated in a different way. Imagine filling up a bathtub to the halfway point with cold water, then pouring in warm water from one side. To begin with there'll be two temperature zones (that's to say, two different energy levels) in the bathtub, which will mix as time passes, eventually resulting in a consistent temperature somewhere between the two.

ENERGY LEVELS IN D4

People with a D4 block normally have a life energy level of 40–50%. They rush from one meeting to the next and are constantly under time pressure. As soon as time starts running out, they become frantic. These people have constant anxiety about missing an appointment, arriving too late, being too old for something, or never achieving anything more in life. This often goes hand in hand with money issues or illnesses that can be described by the component 'time.'

In the second illustration below, the person on the right, who is in D1–D3, has *gained* 15% life energy from the person on the left in D4, who has *lost* 15% in energy. In accordance with the MindFlow Method, the number of people with D1–D3, as well as D4 blocks, represents 85% of all humans.

Energy levels in D4

D4	D1–D3
50%	20%

Δ	–15%	+15%
Σ	35%	35%

ENERGY LEVELS IN D5

People who can take themselves into D5 have very often received 'instructions' or teaching on how to develop themselves spiritually. As explained in the previous chapters, D5 is situated outside of Einstein's spacetime (R4). People in D5 have up to 60% life energy, or can produce up to this level.

In the illustration below, the person in D5 (on the left) has lost, or given, 20% of their energy to the person on the right while interacting with them (here, that person is in D1 and therefore has only 20% energy). The person on the right has doubled their energy, which is reflected in an improved sense of wellbeing.

Energy levels in D5

D5	D1–D4
60%	20%

Δ	-20%	+20%
Σ	40%	40%

ENERGY LEVELS IN D6

People who make it to D6 have long-term spiritual training and practice behind them. They can influence others with psychological programs and subsequently help them, but they can also do damage. These people seem able to manipulate anything and anyone in such a way that everything can be altered according to their wishes and tastes. Their energy level is up to 70%.

The following rhyme applies to them: 'I want! It's a powerful word; say it softly and quietly so it can't be heard. The stars are torn from Heaven by one word: I *want*...' Mental training and psychological programming fall into this realm. Fewer than 5% of people are in D6.

In the next illustration the 'magician' (represented by the magician's hat) who makes it to D6 has done good work (both they and the 'client' believe), as the client has more than doubled their life energy while the magician has conceded less than half of their energy. They can, therefore, carry on with the 'work.'

Energy levels in D6

D6	D1–D4
70%	20%

Δ	-25%	+25%
Σ	45%	45%

However, and this is the tragedy and the risk that many healers take, the magician's energy level will be depleted as time goes by because they have no opportunity to 'fill up' on fresh energy as long as they continue to work on the D6 level, as they're not gaining access to G4.

ENERGY LEVELS IN D7 AND D8

In D7 and D8 we find avatars or the spiritually awakened. The number of people in D7 and D8 is very low. These dimensions are very risky for the people concerned, because all dimensions can drain energy. Therefore, many avatars and spiritually awakened people isolate themselves and become hermits to maintain their high levels of energy.

The next illustration reveals this dangerous situation. The person starts at 99% (D8), but through contact with a person at 40% (D1–D4) it decreases to 69.5%, whereby their energy level drops sharply and the person very quickly ends up in a D5 block. A large increase or decrease in energy can always trigger energetic and physical processes. It's easy to imagine the physical changes that would follow from a stark decrease in energy.

Conversely, the path of the person from D1–D4 is the opposite. Their energy rises suddenly from 40% to 69.5%, meaning the person is 'catapulted' into D5! In this instance, too, it's possible to surmise the physical changes.

Energy levels in D7 and D8

D8	D1–D4
99%	40%

Δ	–29.5%	+29.5%
Σ	69.5%	69.5%

ENERGY LEVELS IN D9

People who manage to enter D9 are in G4 and are therefore in a state that ensures – through Not-Doing and Not-Wanting – all blocks are resolved and can be converted into life energy. In the best-case scenario, interactions with non-G4 people end in complete resolution of their blocks. From G4, these blocks are filled up with pure life energy to a level of 100%!

And here's the special thing about this set-up: The person in G4 also increases their energy level in the process, instead of losing energy as they would at the lower dimensions. Both people benefit from an exchange like this.

In the illustration opposite, the ill person on the right, whose energy is at 20% (so up to 80% blocked), meets a person in D9/G4 with an energy level of 100%. An energetic interaction, which is *not* actively triggered, results in a complete dissolution of the 80% block and a replenishment of 100% life energy from G4.

In my experience, a quarter of the previously blocked energy flows to a person in G4. In our example, a G4 person therefore achieves 120% energy. (In G4, the energy level can rise far beyond 100%.) It's an absolute win-win situation in which the closed system of both people is lifted by the presence of the person on the left in G4.

Energy levels in D9

D9	D1-D4
100%	20%

Δ	+20%	+80%
Σ	120%	100%

If a third person is also involved in a similar set-up, it might look like the following:

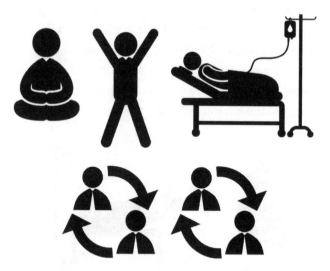

Interaction between people with differing energy levels

Person 1 in D9/G4		Person 2 in D1–D8		Person 3 in D1–D4
100%	1. Interaction: Person 1 with Person 2	40%		20%
Δ +15%		Δ +60%		Δ +0%
∑ 115%		∑ 100%		∑ 20%
Δ +5%		+20%	2. Interaction: Person 2 with Person 3	+80%
∑ 120%		∑ 120%		∑ 100%

Analogous to the previous illustration, in this set-up, the middle person initially meets the person on the left in D9/G4 and tops up their life energy level to 100%. If the middle person now meets a person in D1–D8 (in the illustration, D1–D4; the lower the dimension, the more effective) after contact with the G4 person, the energy flow continues without the middle person having a clue about G4. This state lasts only for a limited time and is dependent on the strength of the nadis of the middle person (*see 'The Nadis,' page 49*).

And the person in G4? They also gain energy in the process. A person in G4 can absorb unlimited energy. In G4, neither the law of the conservation of energy nor a limit on the energy level applies. Energy levels can be topped up without limits. By reaching D9, you've arrived in G4. The dimensions D10–D12 can be reached only by people specially trained in G4 techniques, so I won't go into more detail about these now.

TESTIMONIAL
Andrea from Straubing, Germany

In the past I was influenced by many patterns and allowed myself to be guided by others. In 2014, when I attended Tom's courses, everything in my life changed. I released all that I'd believed up to that point was right and good – whether it was angels or ascended masters – because they were projections of myself. I learned not to take every piece of external information at face value, and to live simply by being. It's as if I've been liberated.

Everything comes from you; everything is presented to you. When you get up in the morning, the day is prepared for you. It's a feeling of absolute freedom. I laugh and dance; I take time for things that previously I'd have thought I wasn't allowed to do.

For me, G4 means doing nothing. It flows. It flows freely. I no longer need to exert myself. There's no longer any effort. It's just the simplicity of being there. I can enjoy people in a completely different way, including my family and my partner.

Chapter 4

G4 – THE CONTROL DIMENSION

According to Maslow's hierarchy of needs, when a person's basic conditions have been fulfilled, they can graduate to the next level of needs. But, as we'll soon see, a person in G4 no longer has needs.

In the state of G4, which encompasses dimensions D9–D12, all energy flows to us. As the dimensions D10, D11, and D12 can be reached only by humans who've been specially trained to do so, D9 is the most relevant dimension in our context. For this reason, we'll equate D9 with G4.

When you're at the spiritual dimension G4, the dimensions of spacetime (D1–D4), as well as the organizational and informational control dimensions (D6–D8), lie below you (so to speak) and all the energy of these lower dimensions flows to you in this moment, topping up your 'energy reservoir.' At D9, or G4, you receive energy 24 hours a day, regardless of where you are. You could walk through a large crowd of people without being jostled by anyone because you're no longer 'resonating' with issues that connote injury, danger, or accidents.

This means that by staying relaxed, and therefore not resonating with blocks, fear, or the stress that comes from an external source in the form of conflicts or risky situations, the associated energy then flows to you – not as an attack or a threat to be fended off, but as pure energy. As a result, tension or resonance disappears, and you can convert the energy from stress or fear into healthy life energy.

Dressage riders who have used MindFlow have discovered that when they enter G4, the horse can sense their relaxation and complies, so they achieve totally different results. A person in G4 is outside the system – everything aligns with them.

You can also observe whether – or how deeply – someone is in G4, and if they're relaxed or not, from their brain frequency or in their emissions, e.g. using a thermal imaging camera.

GOOD AND BAD ENERGY?

Some people may say things like: 'There's negative energy in this room,' or 'That man is giving off really bad vibes!' Well, let me put it this way – this is a good thing as it means a lot of power is present!

In thermodynamics, the law of the conservation of energy doesn't distinguish between good and bad energy. In his calculations, Heim always found only one thing: energy. For example, the energy of electrical current remains constant, regardless of whether it comes from a solar power plant or a nuclear power station; regardless of whether it was generated with good or bad intent.

For the user, electricity is always energy that, for example, makes a lamp light up. When you turn on your lamp, it'll shine just as brightly and consume the same amount of power regardless of whether you curse the electricity or praise it with a Hail Mary.

Energy is neutral, neither good nor bad. You can't use energy to harm someone, either. This only happens when your counterpart 'resonates' with it – so, if they (more or less unconsciously) 'want' to be damaged. For example, when you feel an icy mood in a room, is it real? Yes! As soon as you want to change something, you'll permanently lose energy. With the knowledge that nobody has to change, that everything and everyone is allowed to be as they are, you'll then ideally perceive an environment like this as a classroom for learning, without feeling like a victim.

It's also fine if someone rejects me and I therefore seemingly (!) receive 'negative' energy from them: I don't need to be loved. (You know how it goes: sympathy is free, envy must be earned.) The other person is allowed to be as they are. Every person has a right to exist and is allowed to exist *just as they are*. This is absolute freedom.

Nevertheless, how I handle energy is my personal responsibility. Let's illustrate it in one image: If I take my car to the car wash and later drive it through the mud, I can't complain to the operator of the car wash and ask for another car wash free of charge.

Here's an important point: The exchange of energy between two people always takes place in a perpetrator-victim set-up. So, what happens if you're attacked by an adversary? Their pent-up energy is supposed to be discharged via you, in order to elicit a reaction from you, which in turn replenishes and increases their energy level because they need your energy to maintain their blocks.

But if you (as the 'defender') are in G4, you'll essentially turn the tables. Energy is taken from the attacker, instead of them taking away energy from you. Since the attacker has little energy, the energy is taken away by the 'defender,' where it's at its greatest: the block. It's resolved, and new life energy later takes its place.

Energy flows toward a person in G4 – in this example, that's you as the person being attacked. Once the victim leaves the stage, the perpetrator loses their role and their power. They no longer act out; they're a 'completely normal person' again. This is how you heal another person.

Healing always means you can only heal yourself: No doctor or drug can heal in the same way that you can. Ultimately, the body heals itself by powering up the system, increasing energy, ensuring well-functioning mitochondria and sending the corrupted cells into apoptosis (cell death), by drinking enough fluids to get rid of the 'waste,' and so on. In this sense, everyone is a healer. Every person is his or her own healer!

Let's now weave in some practical exercises:

EXERCISE: THE ZERO-POINT POSITION

Stand up and position yourself as you normally would. Can you feel the tension in your body? People always go after those who are tense. In order to avoid such 'attacks,' you should relax.

To do this, stand with your legs a little further apart than usual, and then hold your right gluteal muscle with your hand, as in the illustration. If it remains slightly tense, move your legs even further apart, *until the gluteal muscle is relaxed*. The gluteal muscle must be relaxed - like in martial arts - otherwise you're weakened and can be overcome by anyone. When the buttocks are tensed, the sciatic nerve – one of the energy pathways – is also pinched.

Also, pay attention to how your solar plexus changes; you'll find it will soften in the zero-point position.

You're welcome to return to standing 'normally' again in order to note the difference, or to repeat the sequence in front of a mirror. Above all, pay attention to how your facial expressions react and the posture of your reflection.

In the zero-point position all energy can flow through the root chakra, making you loose-limbed and relaxed. When you're standing in the zero-point position, you're no longer provoking a reaction, and as a result nobody will attack you or react to you.

The following exercise is believed to absorb the energy from situations.

EXERCISE: ABSORB YOUR ATTACKER'S ENERGY

The more energy your counterpart actually wants to put into his 'attack,' the more energy flows to you and the more potential you'll have at your disposal! Armed with this knowledge, you may find that during an attack you'd like to be yelled at even louder, confronted, and attacked even more, because the energy is no longer directed against you but simply flows into your system. This feels like a warm wind.

Hold your right palm open in front of you and place your left palm on your thigh, as in the illustration. The right palm absorbs energy, while the left palm allows the energy to circulate in your system. When you feel warmth, you've received the energy; you can absorb it and channel it into your own system. Buddha is often depicted with this hand position. The right palm faces upward; the left palm lies on the thigh.

If you want to use this technique while sitting down, without your 'attacker' noticing, turn your right palm upward at the very least - your fingertips should still be pointing forward - or lay your hand open as if you're receiving something in it. Once you engage, you absorb part of the person's energy.

THE 'TROUBLE' PLAYING FIELD

In the lower dimensions of R4 (spacetime, consisting of D1–D4), you're on the 'Trouble' playing field. You're in G3 and can be described through length, width, height, time, and so on, and therefore, numerology and astrology also work in these dimensions. But the moment you switch to G4, you lose these limitations.

Let's imagine a playing piece on this G3 'playing field.' If the piece switches to G4 and thereby leaves the playing field, the maximum stress occurs exactly at this point in the system because something is no longer there that could previously have been described by numbers, i.e. it 'existed' in G3.

What happens if the figure 'falls' from D9/G4 downward through the dimensions? It re-emerges. And where was the overall focus of the system the whole time? It was always on this figure. Now it's returned and has charged itself up with plenty of energy during its 'stay' in G4. To how many people from the system, who have much less energy, is such an energetically charged person interesting? To all, of course!

Here's another example to illustrate the point: A thin piece of paper appears two-dimensional to us; it has a length and a width. Therefore, this piece of paper exists in D1 and D2, but not in D3 (height) and it can't step outside the two-dimensional world. By taking a pen, which is three-dimensional (D1, D2, and D3), from outside and writing on this paper, something new appears on the (two-dimensional) paper that was created by the (three-dimensional) pen, although the 'pen' can't be recognized by the two-dimensional paper from D1 and D2.

This is exactly the kind of magic that we operate from G4 – attention is drawn to the paper because suddenly something is happening. In this moment the system is changing; something is happening.

Let's go a step further. Imagine a piece of paper covered in squares. You're one of these squares, and another square wants to take energy from you. This is exactly how it works in G3. Lines are drawn, so to speak, between the individual squares; these stand for the flow of energy that connects us to one another. When you now go into G4, and are thus outside of the system, you erase this connecting line and consequently change the system. A system can only be changed from the outside. This is difficult to describe; in fact, Heim dedicated his working life to this challenge.

The square that was connected with the other square is exposed to the maximum amount of stress because something that was previously there has now gone. And this square will now do everything in its power to reinstate this line as quickly as possible.

In this situation your goal as an 'outsider' in G4 is not to let any more energy be taken away from others. This is your task. It's all about you; the most important person in your life is yourself! With this approach, you're free. Once you go into G4, everyone else has to adapt to you. This is the change of system. Consequently you leave the 'Trouble' playing field and can no longer be attacked by your former 'fellow players.'

On this subject, here's an exercise to do in pairs.

EXERCISE: TOUCH FOREFINGERS

Stand opposite another person with your raised right index fingers touching (as shown in the illustration). The moment your partner presses his index finger against yours and wants something from you, it's almost inevitable that you'll press back against it, and a test of wills begins.

But if instead you say to yourself, *I don't care what they do*, and remain calm, the other person can work away at you perpetually with their index finger yet you'll withstand the pressure easily; you'll have them under your control the whole time and will gain energy from them. What's more, you're taking away their blocks in the process.

If you (the 'attacked') adopt the approach that the other person is allowed to exert pressure – *He's allowed to do this!* – you offer no resistance, and the attacker quickly loses his power; the attacker is taken over by your relaxed state. At this moment, a reconciliation takes place, and healing begins. Energy flows, the blocks break down. You (as the 'attacked') have the energy, and the attacker has recharged his energy.

This is the effect of the MindFlow Method. There are no losers in this process – there are only two winners. One takes away the other's blocks and gains energy as a result. In fact, both parties see an increase in energy!

In one of my seminars, a bodybuilder with powerful upper arms and a slight woman weighing barely 100lb (45kg) faced each other in this way. Normally the man would have been able to lift up the woman instantly, but because she was in G4, he couldn't move her. Afterward he lay on the floor laughing. The woman had gained energy from him because she wasn't in a state of resistance. The more he'd exerted himself, the more energy she'd gained.

ETHICS

The world should be peaceful but not meek. We should show humility to others without crawling on the floor in front of them. Every human has infinite value. Moreover, one of my guidelines is: 'Ill-gotten gains never prosper.'

To me, 'manipulation' is energy that you actively emit yourself. This means that you suddenly have less energy available, and as a result, you 'vibrate' more slowly and are more vulnerable to energies on a low vibration. Low vibrations might include theft, looting, or cheating. An extremely low vibration is murder. Or, to give some less extreme examples: rows, relationship struggles, and anything else that causes stress. When someone is vibrating very slowly, they accumulate very heavy energy around them, which they attract like a magnet.

As soon as someone is vibrating on a very high level, this high vibration also acts like a magnet. In our work this is, however, not earthly energy, but energy directly from G4. In this state everything you do is energetically accelerated, i.e. put into a faster, higher vibration.

Let's assume you're addressing various issues. The more of these issues you have, the less breathing room you have to live. As soon as certain issues within you are resolved, you gain some breathing space. And, as I mentioned earlier, 'life will then become boring.' Of course, it doesn't really become boring as this breathing space is refilled, albeit with much more useful and meaningful things. But at the beginning, life can actually feel a little empty, as your time is no longer filled with stressful situations and conflicts.

Once you're in this state, you're also no longer dependent on outside help. Instead, you're able to be of help to others, albeit with one big difference – you'll no longer lose any energy in the process. You'll even regain some of the energy you release in other humans. Once you're open and free, nobody will want anything from you. You'll have no energetic blocks and therefore no more issues that other people could resonate with. People will then align themselves with you.

Recently I was asked, 'How can I explain how G4 works to my nephew so that he can get a better bachelor's degree?' Let me get right to the point: If you want to intervene in others' lives, there are two criteria. Look into the palm of your left hand, and if, contrary to expectation, 'God' is written on it, you may intervene halfway; if 'God' is also written on the palm of your right hand, you have free rein to get involved.

But seriously: Who gave you the right to intervene in another person's life? There's only one reason for this kind of intervention – the person in question wishes to exert power over another's life! This even applies to raising children. Many people say: 'Yes, but I have to teach my child to wear rain boots in bad weather. I have to actually raise my child!' But you could also say: 'It doesn't really matter if they walk barefoot through puddles; if they want to, then why not?!' There's an art to not interfering, to not doing anything, to not exerting power over others.

In recent months, a large number of books describing something similar have appeared, dealing with questions such as 'How do you organize people whom you don't lead?' and 'How do people develop and get moving?' The answer is, we do so by giving them free rein. We can compare this to growing a tree: Trees grow beautifully without our help, yet once we start pruning them, we have to continue for the rest of their lives to ensure they grow optimally.

It's necessary to accept that every person has the absolute right to freedom. It's only when every person is taking care of themselves and each individual is doing well that nobody will need to worry about and care for others.

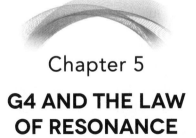

Chapter 5

G4 AND THE LAW
OF RESONANCE

As soon as I broadcast that I can't do something – that I have too little power, that I don't have this, that I'm not loved or respected enough, that I'm misunderstood, and so on – I receive this exact energy in return.

In G4, on the other hand, I have no symptoms of deficiency. The system fills up: It generates an energy field around me in which I don't emit a deficiency. If I stop feeling like a victim, stop broadcasting the fact that I need money or am poor, I won't become a 'perpetrator.' In G4 I know that I have enough love, and as a result I receive enough love.

THE CYCLE OF GIVING AND RECEIVING

It's not wise to earn money without returning anything to the cycle. The aim isn't to collect and hoard one's own energy, to be stingy, but rather to keep everything in motion, always feeding the cycle. In that way, energy also comes back. As soon as you let go, 'it' can flow. To receive something back, you first need to release something (i.e. give something of yourself).

A person who gives nothing won't be able to accept anything. Therefore, if someone attacks you, you may use the energy that the other person gives off in the form of blocks. The attacker comes with a gift for you. They're secretly saying: 'I have a problem. I have lots of energy for you. Can you help me?'

We normally jettison the gift and think, *What a nerve – they're attacking me!* We wince, and the attacker takes our energy. As soon as you've taken an attacker's energy from them, they'll no longer wish to engage aggressively with you. Not because you've conquered them, but because their block will have gone.

The moment it's resolved, the two people can deal with each other without becoming entangled, without putting on a show or acting out a drama, and without needing to feel cooler, smarter, or dumber than the other person.

STRESS REACTIONS

Within the field of epigenetics, research is being carried out to see whether stressed people undergo changes to parts of their genes, which are in turn passed down to their children. As their parents were unable to handle stress, children can be stressed without having been exposed to stress themselves.

In an experiment at the Fraunhofer Institute in Munich, mice were placed under stress through food withdrawal and sleep deprivation. Although the offspring of these stressed mice grew up without these stressors, they still had a shorter lifespan than the comparison group. However, the genes of the offspring were also able to regress to their original state if the environmental or living conditions were correspondingly good.

In this chapter I'll describe some scenarios and return to the same point repeatedly to illustrate the effect of giving an appropriate reaction in G4, instead of being checkmated by a stressor. Power is always given to those who don't utilize it. What of the one who presents him- or herself to the outside world as someone of power, and who seems powerful to many? In fact, there's nobody more *powerless*.

Of course, we've acquired reactions in which our blood pressure rises because we go into a 'flight' reaction; however, it's easy to learn not to suppress these reactions – or to not have them at all – because they aren't worth it.

Reports of horrific incidents and danger lead people to tense up and lose energy. This only serves the system that wants to keep us susceptible to manipulation. According to the media, we always need to be kept in the loop, and *everything* should stress us out: rising energy prices, mounting living costs, ranting politicians... And? Are these *your* problems? No, so don't make them into a problem! A calm and relaxed person achieves better results than someone who quickly loses their composure.

ATTACKS

Attacks are one of the things that cause the most stress, and a lot of energy is required when people defend themselves during attacks. We attack when we have no energy. Bosses notoriously suffer from a lack of energy; they have to lead the company, are always on the go and often traveling for business. They then come into the office and seek somebody out – they think they need energy from others to survive. The lower the life energy, the higher the potential for blocks, which I nonetheless also consider to be energy.

If you enter G4 on a crowded subway train – where lots of people are in D1–D4 – and you smile, you'll experience others moving away slightly because they perceive that something's changed. The person in G4 on the subway receives the energy of others – they take away others' blocks with a smile, and then the corners of many other mouths turn upward too.

Perhaps you've seen the short film *Merci! (Bodhisattva on Metro)* by Christine Rabette on YouTube. In it, a person begins to laugh on the subway, and eventually everyone begins to laugh. This is how blocks are resolved. However, not everyone wants to lose their blocks – because then they have nothing left to hold on to. People have become used to their blocks and are subsequently not always prepared to let them go.

Imagine that you become the subject of an outburst of anger – this means somebody wants to blame you. In 'normal life' an outburst of rage is useful for the person experiencing it; it's a way for them to gain energy. The general rule, however, goes: The attacked (that's you!) has more energy than the attacker. A person in D4, for example, won't attack somebody who is in D2 because the 'D2-er' has less energy.

You could even pat yourself on the back if you're attacked, because you obviously have more energy than the other person. This thought alone could help you emerge from the stress caused by the attack. But because you take a defensive attitude, you're not aware of this and you feel bad.

Examples of Attack and Stress Reactions

In personal, everyday life you'll encounter many situations that you could perceive as an attack or as stress; here are some examples:

- If you don't like the person sat in the seat next to you, he'll receive energy from you, and then he's more likely to move even closer. If instead you adopt an 'I don't care' attitude, even if your seat neighbor smells unpleasant, he'll gradually move away from you.

- What happens when you say: 'I want to feel better – this headache needs to go away *right now*!'? The pain hits even harder because you perceive it as a threat – you're increasing the block because you want to have all the stress that's set in motion. Conversely, if you understand that even your illness is fair enough, then it's able to heal.

- 'Diplomatic' people – those who prefer not to speak their minds or who get 'hot under the collar' because they don't express their anger – often accumulate energy around the neck. And, above all, women who've been told by society to keep their mouths shut have a problem here. An ill-functioning throat chakra leads to inflamed tonsils and is a literal encouragement to (finally) express oneself.

For those of us who like to compromise and create peace, there's the danger that we give away something of ourselves to ensure that another person keeps their mouth shut – so that they remain civil, and even so that they stay with us! But this is counterproductive, because the moment we leave the (attacking) energy of the other person with them and don't take it, we are reinforcing their block and saying: 'This attack is fine, you can repeat it any time!' The correct solution is not to react to this attack. Then, something crazy happens: You'll feel a warm sensation; you'll feel the energy flowing through you and know that you have more power.

THE ENERGY CURVE

Many people engage with their energy in the way shown in this graph:

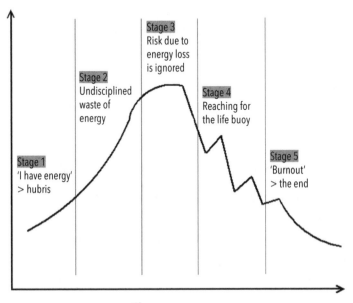

The energy curve

Stages of the Energy Curve

Stage 1: You think you have plenty of energy. This is critical; it may be when hubris begins – yes, you have energy, you can work with others, you can heal others, you can *give energy to others...*

Stage 2: Undisciplined waste of energy – 'I have enough energy, everything's working, we're handling this easily.'

Stage 3: The danger of energy loss is ignored. You're driving along a cliff, so to speak, and you forget that the end is ahead of you. There's extreme danger of falling!

Stage 4: Reaching for the life buoy. You look for someone who can energetically treat and rescue you. The energy curve briefly goes upward, but then drops off again.

Stage 5: Burnout. The body has produced so many stress hormones that it can no longer break them down.

Handling Energy

Burned-out managers and chief executives often come to my practice. Some of them earn millions, but what we don't always consider is that they often don't talk to anyone about stress. They're not allowed to show weakness, and they always have to be the best at everything. They're permanently stressed. The burnout stage forces them to start all over again and to learn to conserve their energy.

The MindFlow Method is very well suited to this kind of situation because we're able to jump over burnout – the external attack – very quickly. The bigger the external attack, the more quickly you can re-emerge from it. In the event of a real attack, lots of energy is flowing. It might sound horrifying, but it's true: The more serious the attack, the more energy in the room.

A person who is genuinely attacking you is giving you something – they're showing you your issues, your blocks – and at the same time, they want you to heal them! But what's your usual reaction? Firstly, you ask yourself: *What did I do wrong?* With this question, however, you're already allowing the initial energy to flow to the attacker. Secondly, you want to improve yourself. Yet as a result, even more energy is being transferred to the other person.

Will your attacker come back to you again next time? Well, of course. As long as they can draw energy from you, they'll spring back like a boomerang, with the effect that you'll become tired because they've gained your energy. This isn't what you want in life. Everyone should keep their energy – there's enough energy available for everyone. This energy permanently accumulates in your system. You receive the energy from the universe and/or from Earth, and the energy from G4 is infinitely available.

We're always trying to be in balance with others. A person in a state of wanting weakens him- or herself! A person who doesn't care about being challenged or attacked by others gains in strength while their opponent becomes weaker. They can no longer be manipulated.

The attacker who wants to 'provoke' someone has a block – they want to defeat the other person; they aren't satisfied with the fact that the other person is, for example, in this position. Even if the person being attacked is physically weaker than the attacker, the attack will not succeed in defeating them as long as the 'attacked' person maintains the attitude that the attack doesn't matter to them. In the context of quantum physics, you might say: The attacked is not (or is no longer) 'entangled' with the attacker.

This experience of not reacting to an attack must be made once, and then the body remembers this state and can recall it again and again if necessary. The body takes all the energy from the attacker – the attacker's block resolves itself, while at the same time his energy is filled up (a feeling of warmth) and his system works more powerfully.

Play with Life Versus Fight with Life

Learn to play with your energy in such a way that you don't lose any energy in the process! 'Play with life' and don't 'fight with life.' How does that work? The art is in Not-Doing, and accepting that another person is there (you'll learn about this in Chapter 6, 'The Concept of Not-Doing'). Then you'll no longer fight. The moment when you do nothing is also when you're no longer vulnerable to external attacks. Wherever you are, and however you deal with others, it's okay – you have no issues with it.

The most vulnerable person in G3 (D1–D8) is the person in D8, as they're suitable as 'food' for everyone. The higher your level of life energy within G3, the more people will cling on to your 'coattails.' With, let's say, 99% life energy, you suddenly become very interesting to everyone in your surroundings. This means that you come under extreme attack and everybody wants energy from you.

I can't repeat it often enough: The more serious the external attack, the greater the gift, as then the more energy you potentially have available! The more energy that's there, the more energy you can trade. In G4, unlimited energy is available!

In the summer of 2017, we held a seminar in the desert in Abu Dhabi in the United Arab Emirates, 25 miles (40km) from the nearest signs of civilization. There we were exposed to the elements. The hotel staff were quite nervous when we went out into the hot desert sand during our lunch break to do our exercises. What happened? Almost all of the participants suddenly felt a chill! The attack by the heat was converted into energy because we were in G4.

Many of the experts I've trained practice ice-bathing. Climbing into ice-cold water is an attack. One can judge it and fear a heart attack as a result of the cold, but anyone who dares to take an ice bath can go into the water and notice how the cold gives them energy.

ACCEPTANCE

Would you like to make an active difference to your surroundings? Then the first question you should ask yourself is: *Why should somebody have to do something for me?* If you have to manipulate this person, it'll reflect on you (*see 'Ethics,' page 87*).

If you're in a state of wanting, these desires only function through the expenditure of your own life energy, and this can negatively affect your strength and, at worst, your body and subsequently, your health.

The solution lies in *not wanting something*; so, rather than attracting something through expending energy and targeting intentions, you should be open and accepting of what awaits you – i.e. you should accept things effortlessly. To begin with, these can be tiny details. You're engaged with the learning process of being able to accept things because you deserve it all. Once you accept and receive something small, the channel will gradually open and the things you're prepared to accept will become greater and greater.

As soon as you imagine something, you limit yourself and lose energy because you're fixating on a defined image. If, on the other hand, you let this image go and place it in the flow of energy, it'll find its way to you. In G4, we're in a state where we don't want anything and can't manipulate anything. Instead of chasing after every thing possible, we *accept* what's coming.

The central question of MindFlow is not what we want to achieve, but rather what we're prepared to accept! It's a complete turnaround. We try to manifest the things that we want, but often we're carrying blocks within us that prevent us from having those very things. But if we practice acceptance, life unfolds before us. Because the divine – or however you wish to refer to it – always has the best in store for us. We just need to be prepared to accept it.

Once you're in G4, you have complete freedom from issues and the ego. In this state your energy system can let go of blocks and new energy from G4 can flow in. In this way you can bring the energies in yourself, as well as in others, back to their original flow.

Let's assume you're prepared to accept success in your professional activities. Don't fixate on your current occupation alone. Perhaps success will come with a job that you'd never previously considered as a possibility. Let the energy flow. When you enter G4, be prepared to accept success, and then pay attention to the signs that show it in your life.

A healer in one of my seminars wanted her practice to be successful so that she could make a living from it. She tried everything, but the flood of patients simply never arrived. But then she began to open up and realized that her true skill lay in holding seminars. Since then she's been leading successful seminars on the treatment techniques she's previously worked with.

Be prepared to accept and seize new opportunities, and this will then become a matter of course for you and all those around you – without envy, without resentment.

You've received something because you were able to accept it – which is something quite different to fighting for something tooth and nail. You saw it as a possibility but you neither deliberately desired it nor directed your intention toward it. You can accept what you saw, and as a result, it has entered your life and will come naturally. Everything necessary for it to be realized will automatically come to you. Life aligns with you as you're in G4.

This is the biggest difference between MindFlow and all other techniques. You'll find more about acceptance in Chapter 12, 'The Power Tool.'

IMPLEMENTATION

What you're able to accept will appear in your life. However, this doesn't mean that it'll fall into your lap by itself. When you let go, opportunities and people will step into your life. This doesn't mean drifting through life without a plan; it definitely requires work, diligence, and discipline. It's like driving a car: If you rush past all the exits on the highway, what might await you there will never come to you. If you can't stop because you're too focused on a goal-oriented desire, you'll not seize opportunities and chances.

You need to pick an opportunity that's ripe. When you're free from blocks and a fixed desire, this can happen easily. Then, however, it's a matter of manifesting and energetically anchoring this opportunity in your G3 space. It's only through your acceptance that you ultimately decide what you receive – this is distinct from what you want. So many possibilities open up before you! It's also no longer a matter of saying: 'I want…' Instead, you say: 'I see… and I accept.'

Of course, sometimes it can go wrong, but that's part of the process and it will have led you to a new dimension that you'd never have reached otherwise. At a moment like this, you'll gain the strengths needed to deal with the situation. This is the intelligence of the G4 consciousness.

Imagine there are 20,000 chocolates in front of you, basically an infinite number of possibilities to choose from. Today, perhaps, you'll plump for a nutty nougat, tomorrow it'll be truffle, and the day after that some other treat. This is the end of limitation. At this point there's no competition and no taking offense. Everything is present in abundance and great diversity.

I'll give you another, entirely quotidian example: Imagine you want to reach a destination but are stuck in a traffic jam that stretches for miles. You could get all worked up about it, become irritated, and put yourself under internal pressure. Or you could remove the pressure and then have time to otherwise occupy yourself, such as by having a conversation with someone using a hands-free phone or contemplating a new project, consequently experiencing something that you would never have encountered otherwise. A new 'engine' suddenly revs into life.

I was once stuck in traffic with my wife. The street was completely blocked due to a serious accident; nothing was moving in either direction. There was a makeshift exit on the right, so we just took that, following our instincts. Eventually we stumbled upon a beautiful lodge where we stopped for a bite to eat and got to know some nice people. The gridlock was still visible on the horizon, but we relaxed and used the opportunity of this downtime for ourselves. We still have good memories of the event to this day (notwithstanding the distressing accident).

G4 AND SWARM INTELLIGENCE

Once many people are in G4, everything takes its course. Nobody needs to worry about anything. Everyone gives energy and receives energy. It's an intelligent process of mutual creation. Everybody is looking at those around them, and everything is intertwined – without direction and without rules.

In G4, each person follows their instincts, and the necessary things and people are attracted; the system keeps itself running. It's simply doing, without intention and ambition behind it. It's the motivation to exist from within oneself, but not outside of one's own destiny. This system follows a cosmic order that's comparable to a shoal of fish or a flock of birds, in which all members move at the same rhythm and in the same direction – because all individuals are in G4 and are connected to one another through this higher consciousness.

TESTIMONIAL
Helga from Munich, Germany

My self-esteem was once pretty dismal and very wobbly. I got upset about every little thing and had essentially checked out of life. Since I've been working with MindFlow, things have improved immeasurably. I'm no longer so sensitive, and many changes have occurred as a result. These affect my private life and my relationship – my partner and I had a very cooperative relationship beforehand, but even in that arena, I now express my opinions much more often.

Much has changed for me at work too. I say what I think there now, in such a way that my colleagues can accept it and not dismiss me as a know-it-all. For example, I had an altercation with a young man who was fuming with anger and ended up standing in front of me with a face as white as a sheet and clenched, raised fists. I thought he was going to punch me in the face. Then I said to myself, *Right, I can't get out of here anymore: I can't escape.* Completely calm and composed in G4, I lowered my gaze and looked at the man's fists, and in that moment he dropped them. It melted away from him as it did from me. He was still loud and angry – completely justifiably, in his view – but he left the room without further argument, without slamming doors. And that day, everything was fine. It was very impressive.

Chapter 6

THE CONCEPT OF
NOT-DOING

In ancient Greek mythology, there are explanations for everything. Let's take Homer's epic poem the *Odyssey* as an example. In it, the hero Odysseus falls into the hands of Polyphemus, a one-eyed giant with immeasurable power who represents the Underworld. How could Odysseus overcome Polyphemus? By calling himself 'Nobody.' As Nobody, he was able to get the better of the underworld, because NOBODY can only do NOTHING.

When Polyphemus's eye was gouged out by Odysseus (Nobody), he cried out to his fellow giants for help, saying that 'Nobody' had blinded him, and 'Nobody' was trying to murder him!' And so it came to pass that the other giants stopped looking for him. Odysseus had done something that should have elicited a reaction. But when you do NOTHING in G4, reactions no longer ensue.

Not-Doing is a balancing act. In 2000 I worked in a company where the meeting culture was strong – there was a meeting held every day. At some point I asked: 'And when will we work…?' Because what is a meeting anyway? Energy goes back and forth, but nothing is put in motion. Instead of a meeting, it's better to be in a state of Not-Doing, and to take matters into your own hands. This sounds like a paradox, but you just have to understand how it works.

They say that the dumbest farmers have the biggest potatoes. This isn't meant maliciously, only that they simply *do* something instead of questioning everything! When we question things, the intellectual mind tells itself that 'XYZ can't be like this.' It wants to control everything. When you switch off your intellect and simply exist, it can work the other way. The moment that you realize you don't have to do anything and can still exist is 'magical' (*see 'The "Trouble" Playing Field,' page 83*). At this point, you're no longer susceptible to manipulation.

Each and every one of us must always act in such a way that we're free – free to do what's necessary. We may say that we're not doing anything in G4, but we do just as much and as little as is necessary.

NOT-DOING AND GAINING EVERYTHING

Let's turn now to a concept that's essential for an intellectual understanding of the MindFlow Method. Once you're in G4, all energy flows toward you. Everything aligns with you. However, this doesn't put you in a position of power from which you can act as you wish. Instead, it's important to exist entirely without intention. In this state, you must end all goal-oriented action.

Why? Because it's only when you take yourself out of the equation that the energy can flow along the correct pathways. Everything will then work in your interest, and much more will ensue than would have been possible in a goal-oriented, egocentric state. Everything is possible, because once you can think of something, the *possibility* of it also exists. It's then merely your decision whether or not to accept it. Everything that you can imagine can manifest for you in this state. How? As everything aligns with you in G4, you'll encounter people, chances, and opportunities that'll bring you to the very point where you can realize this possibility.

The principle is as follows: Adopt Not-Doing and gain everything, with Not-Doing meaning the elimination of all intentional and goal-oriented behavior. There's still work to be done in the earthly sense, so it's not about 'doing nothing,' but about *Not-Doing in the sense of acting without intention.*

In the following chapters, you'll learn the essential techniques to help you reach G4 and allow you to increase your energy. For it to work, however, two conditions must first be met:

1. You must be in a condition of total acceptance. Touch your solar plexus. If it's relaxed, then your attitude is correct.

2. You must be aware that *everything is energy*. Even your blocks and limitations are energy – albeit blocked energy, but still energy that can be brought back into flow. Revisit Chapter 3, 'The Energy Levels,' *(see page 63)* for a reminder of how this works.

HANDLING OTHERS' DEMANDS AND EXPECTATIONS

In your everyday life, you're almost certain to have to deal with people who expect things of you – those who have an agenda regarding you and consequently want something from you. There are two levels to dealing with such demands and expectations:

1. The Level of Acceptance

Here, you accept others' expectations and fulfill them with joy, consistency, and all of your energy. Once you're no longer in negative resonance, e.g. at work in relation to your boss, energy will flow, and the tasks assigned to you will be a piece of cake.

The much more important issue behind this, however, is that you'll be receiving energy from your boss as a consequence. Your boss wants you to do something and you go into G4 and say, smiling: 'I'd love to. Can I help with anything more?' The energy of 'wanting' and the 'needing-to-do' that your boss radiates thus flows into your system and increases your energy level.

It's similar to being of service – serving another person is free and brings love and appreciation to the one serving in this consciousness. However, the principle of acceptance does not by implication mean having to do everything and serving others like a butler – once you're in G4, this will no longer happen, but for the sake of completeness, we've mentioned it here. Because if someone makes such an attempt, the person who wants something from you will lose their energy and release it to you.

2. Enter G4, Smile, and the Energy Flows to You

At this level, the other person will ask themselves: *What did I actually want? What was it that I just wanted?* Their energy is then with you and it flows into your system. The person wanted something from you, and this desire strengthened your energetic position. The 'attacker's' block resolved and you both benefit from that. This is the basic order.

There are numerous ancient accounts of masters in Asian sword combat who stood opposite one another for hours without making a move. As they both knew, whoever moves opens up a loophole, and their attacking energy can be used against them. This principle applies in other types of martial arts, such as Aikido and Wing Chun, as well as for Qigong masters who redirect the attacking energy of the opponent and are able to use it against the attacker themselves.

The same principle underpins the MindFlow Method. In using it, all routes are open to you; you can go in all directions, so to speak. Every route is the right one if it comes from within yourself. There's no intention and no wanting; rather, only an acceptance of new directions and new possibilities that ensue as a result of the G4 consciousness.

UNLEARNING 'HELPER SYNDROME'

You could care about everybody and his dog, but then you'll be carting around a great deal of baggage. If you've ever walked the Camino de Santiago (a network of pilgrim routes in Europe) you'll have realized that next time it would be better to set off with minimal luggage, taking only the bare necessities.

The lighter the load and the fewer entanglements one has, the better. I can't feel responsible for everybody – that would be beyond my means. Some healers become sick because they just give, give, give. But it's not about becoming 'less,' reducing one's energy and always giving – it's about reducing one's load. (*For more information on attempting to solve others' concerns, see 'Ethics,' page 87*).

Herbert from Linz, Austria

Since I've been working with the MindFlow Method, I find I'm not afraid much anymore. Before, I had many patterns and mental structures that I've now completely lost. I simply no longer need them. On the other hand, I've become much more sensitive and have a heightened sense of empathy.

Last year, I took the car ferry to the island of Crete in Greece. I couldn't sleep so I went up onto the deck at 1 a.m. At the very top I took a seat, made myself comfortable, and gazed up at the sky. And then I spotted a man standing right on top of the railings. I thought to myself: *Is he about to jump?* I didn't react and just stayed sitting where I was.

All of a sudden, the man called out to me: 'Can't you see you're interrupting?' I replied: 'I don't know what you mean. I won't bother you while you're jumping. It's your decision. If you jump down there, I won't call for help. I won't do anything.'

I was very surprised that I stayed so cool in that moment. And then one thing led to another. An hour later we were sat next to each other drinking a bottle of wine, and the story was in the past.

I'd never had that feeling before, despite practicing psychotherapy for 35 years and completing 14 different qualifications. As a result, it was something really quite significant. MindFlow works without my intention.

Chapter 7

THE MINDFLOW METHOD

MindFlow won't teach you how to dominate, oppress, or win others over: We don't want to produce any losers because in situations with a loser, the energy isn't balanced. Instead, working in G4 results in a win-win situation. As soon as someone loses a block, they've experienced healing. In our work every participant should always emerge from situations with more energy.

With MindFlow no energy transfer takes place: rather, we ensure that our own energy can develop to its fullest. Then the individual standing wave emitted by every person is at its optimum, and we can receive what's due to us – without effort, and without having to do anything.

So, just as every person has their own energy field, every person also has their own *learning* field. As soon as you understand that, you can deal with attacks differently. I don't have to take it personally when somebody thinks I'm dumb. All I can do is deal with it. I could preserve the attack and keep it going for the next 10 years, but I can also send it toward its healing.

RESOLVING ENERGY BLOCKS

At its core, MindFlow is about resolving blocks, both your own and those of others. Interestingly enough, even if they've accompanied people for years, blocks can simply dissolve in the MindFlow process.

As you now know, everyone has blocks. Some have been there since birth, while others have been acquired. If we don't process our blocks, the law of resonance comes into play and enlarges them. The MindFlow Method, however, puts you in a state of G4 within seconds, and the block is 'churned up' and drains away.

As you can see in the illustration opposite, the mind is located in the intellect: 'The mind is willing, but the flesh is weak.' The mind does what I tell it. If I tell it to stay sane, it will carry out this order.

All of our problems, worries, and physical pains are blocks; they're usually located in the nervous system. I refer to them as 'sparrows on a wire,' and I compare the nervous system to guitar strings.

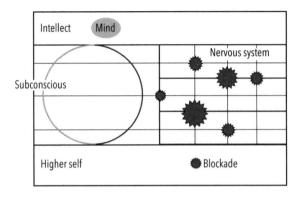

The mind is located in the intellect

As soon as we enter G4, the liberated mind returns to its origin, namely the higher self (see illustration below). In so doing, it brushes the guitar strings, essentially 'stroking' the nervous system.

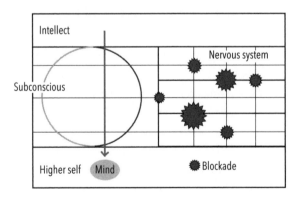

The mind returns to the higher self

The sparrows on the wire feel a shock for the first time. The more frequently you do this, the sooner the first sparrow will fall off the wire. With each stroke, one or two sparrows fall down. Nonetheless, please note that it's not necessarily the sparrow that you would like to see fall, for as soon as you look at a particular sparrow, hoping to get rid of it, you're once again nourishing it with energy… and keeping it put. But if you say: 'I don't care which sparrow falls,' then the biggest sparrow might fly away.

Or imagine you're cutting up an onion. The thickest, toughest, and dirtiest layers are on the outside. The further in you go, the thinner and more delicate the layers become. The same applies when resolving blocks – the more deeply we penetrate, the subtler and more delicate the blocks become.

Even I personally still have blocks, and I don't spend the whole day in G4; nonetheless, I'm mostly in G4, which can be stressful for other people to begin with because they're confronted with their own blocks as a result. But after a while, they begin to seek me out because of their unconscious desire to resolve these blocks.

When I use energy to defend myself against manipulation and attacks, or to put up resistance, I feel bad. Consider this: 'I don't want them to attack me' will increase my instability, rather than my stability. However, if I take the 'I don't care what they do to me' point of view, the other person will have to make a huge effort to move me and will lose energy. Their attack drifts into my stability. Therefore, if someone attacks or yells at me while I remain in this confident position, I become more and more stable.

It always depends on how I react to the other person – on my attitude. As long as I'm rebelling against myself, the other person's attack will hurt me. If instead I think, *Let them do it!*, the other person isn't given the satisfaction of taking action against me.

Perpetrator-Victim Set-Up

To repeat: This is about a 'victim' and a 'perpetrator.' If the victim no longer sees him- or herself as a victim and leaves the stage, the perpetrator will remain there alone. The show ends. As there's no longer a victim, the perpetrator no longer has a task. Then the perpetrator is hitting something that doesn't exist.

It's the same in all areas of life. Consider this: In which part of your life do you feel like a victim? The moment you stop fighting, you have the opportunity to get everything. A person taking a punch with their right hand can no longer take anything with that hand; so they have no chance of receiving something from others. With MindFlow, however, you go through life with open hands.

Whoever I meet may give me everything. They may give me gifts, attack me, get angry with me, criticize me, and insult me. When someone attacks me, they're actually giving me a gift. They're serious; they approach me with all of their anger, and they really mean it. They're not one of the sneaks who outwardly praise me but then stab me in the back. They give me their life energy – but then it's up to me to take it and give them the therapy, as it were, by saying: 'Okay, you don't have to do this with me anymore. I get it – it's all good.'

The moment I no longer need to represent anything – when I have no block, and when I can accept everyone as they are – my opponent will no longer be able to 'entangle' me. As soon as the perpetrator wants to attack me, I make my exit as a possible victim and say: 'Sorry, not me!' It's as if I were to say to you: 'Come on, let's beat each other up now,' and you reply: 'Right, get outside, Tom, and start bleeding; I'll follow.' Then there will be no more entanglements.

INCREASING ENERGY

I had a friend with a stutter and he always needed a long time to express himself. One day, while we were in a group together, he had to explain something in detail, and I knew that it would take some time. I went into G4 and said to him: 'Oh dear, this may take a while.' He looked at me, and the rest of the group, and started laughing. And from that moment on his block vanished – he never stuttered again.

How is that possible? Imagine a lump of ice – frozen water, hard and immobile. Then you open a door (which corresponds to raising the energetic frequency to G4) so the sun can shine in, and the lump of ice begins to melt. The rigid structure has dissolved into water and is now able to move. The water can flow freely.

Let's continue with this metaphor. With continuous sun exposure, i.e. staying in the field of G4, the water can evaporate and thus, unlike ice or water in liquid form, it can move freely in the air. Consequently, the energy isn't just in free flow, it's everywhere. The water vapor penetrates through doors, windows, and all objects. The possibilities increase, and life literally takes place on a new level. And it gets even better: Anyone who has resolved another person's blocks receives some of the liberated energy directly into their system, which in turn lifts them to a higher energy level and exponentially enhances their capabilities; they go from warm water vapor to hot water vapor, as it were.

In summary, we can therefore say that the lump of ice corresponds to the blocks in dimensions D1–D4; it begins to melt, which is the energetic equivalent of D5–D8. As soon as the water evaporates, we're in D9–D12, i.e. on the level of G4. Which, of course, would never be possible as a 'block of ice.' If we stay with our image, in G4 you can be everywhere and penetrate through every crack, even the narrowest bottleneck; you can resonate everywhere!

Here's a little everyday story to clarify this idea. You might stand in an elevator like a block of ice, looking at the floor and hoping that nobody will recognize you. Or you could try a different approach and take away the blocks of the nervous elevator users. When I enter an elevator, I sometimes jump up and down briefly on the spot and say: 'Oh, hopefully it'll hold!' Of course, you have to be able to 'take' it if someone jumps down your throat as a result of doing this, because 220lb (100kg) does cause a certain vibration in the elevator. Usually, however, my 'thawing' remark acts as an entrée to a short and enjoyable conversation.

Real-Life Examples

Once, two youngsters were brought to my practice by their mother because they were regularly being beaten by their father. I showed the children the asanas (coming up in the next chapter), which they used to enter G4. The result? The father never mistreated them again.

Why was this? When the father grabbed or hit the children, he actually wanted to be close to them. This was a block held by the father. But as soon as the children stopped resonating with the father's block, he kept his hands off them because he would have lost energy as a result. These kinds of people only go where they can get energy, never where they lose energy.

There's an important lesson for us all here. It goes: *The weaker person always goes after the stronger person in order to gain energy from them.* From an energetic point of view, anyone who is attacked is in the stronger position. Interestingly, this also implies that in victim-perpetrator configurations, the 'victim' has more energy than the 'perpetrator,' but the former allows this energy to be stolen from them.

A friend of mine owns a boutique in Stuttgart, Germany, and her employees were often harassed by a man who exposed himself – to the extent that they no longer wanted to work there. She came to me for advice, and I suggested that the next time the man entered the shop, she should shout at him: 'Want a fuck? I'd be up for it!'

She did this, and as a result the man never reappeared. Why? It was no longer fun for him because he didn't elicit a reaction. The issue was solved in one attempt. And believe me, that man's lost his blocks; he's done with this issue, and he'll never harass anyone in this way again.

DEALING WITH ENERGY

When you're annoyed, you automatically emit energy. Is it worth it? The next time you're feeling annoyed, look around you – someone will start to smile, namely the one who is receiving the energy.

I once flew into Basel airport and there was only one border guard checking a very long line of passengers from four planes. The atmosphere was quite 'charged.' An older Frenchman was standing in front of me, and initially he was very tense. After a while he handed his backpack to his wife and said loudly: 'When we come to passport control, *you* take the drugs!'

Everyone around him laughed. Why? He'd evidently absorbed the strong energy in the room, and now he could have fun. It set the whole environment in motion. (Warning – you can't make these kinds of statements at every airport!)

When you resolve blocks in another person, energy flows to you and that makes you very powerful. And yet it's by no means the case that the other person suffers: Quite the opposite, in fact, because they lose their block. It's a win-win situation – both parties benefit. For this reason I strongly recommend that you stop maintaining the blocks of others, and instead try to resolve them. You'll both benefit.

During my seminars, I'm by no means the 'nice guy'; sometimes I really challenge and provoke the participants. However, they know exactly why I take this approach – to help them release their blocks. I can handle their reactions. If someone says to me: 'Tom, you're the biggest a**hole in the world!' I'll counter with: 'You're right. Go ahead, sock it to me!' And by that, I mean: 'Feel free to rant at me; please give me more of your energy, because I don't think that was enough.'

Once you know what this will trigger, you're allowed to question *everything* on one condition – you must first enter G4 and be able to endure and accept what comes next! Say to yourself: *No matter what is heading my way, it's energy and I'll enjoy this energy.*

Three key points

1. Entering G4 consciousness is the name of the game. What you then say or ask is of secondary importance; the energetic attitude from which you do it is more important.

2. If you want to hurt or discredit the other person, it won't work; that would be the first mistake. You need to address the question to your counterpart in a totally neutral stance, free from any opinion or emotion.

3. The second mistake would be to take the reaction of your counterpart personally, because then you'll have lost too.

Keep the three points above in mind as you read the following example:

A woman who'd experienced a great deal of harassment came to my practice. I could, of course, have taken care of her blocks, worked through her traumas and strengthened her in her suffering, grief, anger, and pain. But instead I only asked her one question, after which everything changed for her. I switched to G4 (the essential requirement!) and asked her: 'And did you enjoy it?'

As a result of my provocative question, all the woman's anger and hatred was discharged in that moment, which meant she let go of her block completely. I simply stood there with open hands and received her energy. She screamed and wept for about five minutes, and then the block was resolved. She was able to accept the experience. She no longer had any conflict with it, the issue was resolved, and she was free again.

What can we learn from this? You're not helping other people by 'nurturing' their blocks; instead, get them to release the blocked energy and at the same time, to let go of the associated trauma. At this point let's weave in an exercise to illustrate this basic approach.

EXERCISE: PIERCING ENERGY BLOCKS

Find someone who has an issue with conflict. For starters, it should be a minor conflict that, importantly, has nothing to do with you. Address the conflict issue without judgment and without intention.

Sit at a table with the person opposite you, and ask them to tell you about their problem, their conflict. Do nothing and simply let the conversation take its course; you're just the audience. (This conversation can, of course, also take place on the phone.)

Raise your right hand (you can do this under the table so that your counterpart can't see it). Now perceive what comes as energy as a warm wind flowing into your system. Your left hand is on your left thigh with the palm facing downward, so that the energy can circulate in your system.

As you'll be able to feel, the energy dissipates relatively quickly and the block dissolves. Observe the way the face or voice of your counterpart changes and how their tension is released.

The moment you feel heat flowing to you, or you sense warmth, you're receiving energy. As soon as you feel cold, you're losing one of your own blocks and the blocked energy is dissolving.

One of my seminar participants takes part in numerous meetings professionally. In meetings, when many ego and power struggles can take place, she holds her right palm under the table, facing the speaker, with her left palm on her thigh. She absorbs the blocks of the participants and increases her own energy as a result.

The interesting thing about this practice is that since she's been doing it, the meetings have become calmer, more focused, and much more relaxed. Initially, the power-hungry 'alpha leaders' lost so much energy during the meetings that they wanted to finish early. They then became calmer and more levelheaded, and as a result, the best solution could be found for everyone involved. And it stayed that way. The managers lost their blocks – not through pithy sayings, but through a subtle, imperceptible flow of energy that loosened and eventually resolved them.

Testimonial
Maria from Ingolstadt, Germany

I do a lot of gardening, and since I've been practicing the MindFlow Method, I've been planting and sowing in the state of G4. This has had an effect on the harvest – the year before last, it was small because voles ate a lot of the produce, but last year, when I planted everything in G4, that didn't happen. The harvest was much bigger, and we had fresh vegetables from the garden all summer. It was really impressive.

Chapter 8
THE ASANAS

The physical exercises featured in this chapter, known in yoga as 'asanas,' will activate the flow of energy within you. The asanas can be used in everyday life to 'assert' yourself in your dealings with others without producing an opponent! So it's not a matter of getting resistance, but rather taking the other person with you into G4. You can do the asanas in any place where there's a lot of power or attacks.

The asanas have a direct impact on the body's nadis (*see page 49*). The more frequently you practice the asanas, the stronger the energy flow in the nadis and the higher their capacity to transport energy.

HOW TO PERFORM THE ASANAS

The asana sequence features five asanas, followed by an exercise to distribute energy, and an exercise to relax your solar plexus. It's best to carry out the sequence twice daily (in the morning and the evening) in the order shown on the following pages. With this practice, you can strengthen your body energetically and enter a state similar to G4.

At first, please ensure that you always practice the asana sequence while facing *east*, because then the Earth will be rotating in your direction; the energy, the Earth's radiation, will flow directly to you and will also bolster your energy system. Try to avoid practicing *at noon*, for as long as the sun is at its highest point, because the Earth's radiation is then pressed down by the sun's radiation and is minimal; this makes the asanas less effective. At night, or at sunrise and sunset, when the sun is at a flat angle, the Earth's radiation is at its strongest and is best absorbed by the asanas.

While performing each asana, keep your eyes open and your knees apart. The more you practice the sequence, the longer the G4 state can develop in your body. The asana sequence should take between two and five minutes to perform and can be easily integrated into daily life. It's a minimal amount of time with a big impact. You'll find a free video tutorial on how to perform the asanas at our website: www.mindflow.academy.

ASANA 1: STANDING FORWARD BEND

This posture ensures good grounding.

Associated chakra: root chakra (1st chakra)

~ The feet are positioned hip width apart.

~ Ensure the knees aren't locked.

~ The upper body and head hang down loosely forward.

~ Breathe through the mouth.

~ The hands must not touch the floor, otherwise the energy will flow out again.

~ The arms can swing gently.

~ The body swings or turns easily.

ASANA 2: THE H POSE

This posture creates a universal circuit, a connection between Heaven and Earth.

Associated chakra: crown chakra (7th chakra)

~   The feet and knees are in a slightly open position.

~   The arms are raised vertically up to the ears.

~   The palms face each other.

~   The head is raised to a '2 o'clock' position, as if looking up at the sun.

~   Breathe through the nose.

~   The energy flows through the hands and arms into the body.

Asana 3: The Y pose

This posture resembles Jesus ascending to Heaven.

Associated chakra: forehead chakra (6th chakra)

~ The feet and knees are together.

~ The arms are stretched out diagonally and raised above the head, like the letter Y (it's important to feel which is the best arm position for you to receive the most energy).

~ The palms are open, as if about to catch a big ball.

~ The hands act like antennae that absorb energy.

~ The head is in the '2 o'clock' position, as if looking up at the sun.

~ Breathe through the nose.

~ The energy comes from the ground and flows upward.

Asana 4: The Priest

This posture is like a priest who is blessing a congregation.

Associated chakra: sacral chakra (2nd chakra)

~   The feet and knees are together.

~   The arms are extended horizontally to the sides with the forearms angled upward.

~   The palms face forward.

~   The head is raised, with the gaze slightly raised.

~   Breathe through the nose.

~   The energy is directed forward.

ASANA 5: THE ROCKET

This posture resembles take off.

Associated chakra: solar plexus (3rd chakra)

~ The feet and knees are together.

~ As you become more experienced at this asana, you can bring the feet into a V position, with heels touching.

~ The head is raised, with the gaze slightly raised.

~ Breathe through the nose.

~ The arms are stretched away from the body at the sides, like wings, and the palms are facing the floor.

~ Coming from below, the energy presses against the hands, like a rocket taking off. The correct arm position is where the most 'lift' is felt.

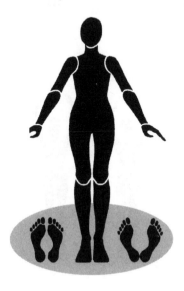

DISTRIBUTING ENERGY

Next, complete this four-part 'distributing energy' exercise three times.

Step 1: Bring the energy up

~ Stand with your legs apart, bend forward, and imagine you are reaching into a pile of feathers lying at your feet. Lift the feathers up over your head.

Step 2: Distribute the energy

~ Use your fingers to pull at the feathers.

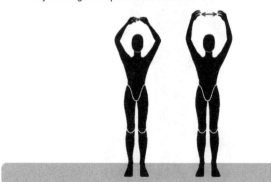

Step 3: Move the energy

~ Spread the feathers over your head by turning your palms forward three times and backward three times.

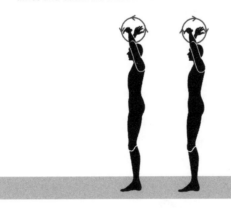

Step 4: Bring the energy down

~ Press your arms down on the left and right side of your body. You should feel a slight coolness on your hands, caused by shedding excess energy from your body.

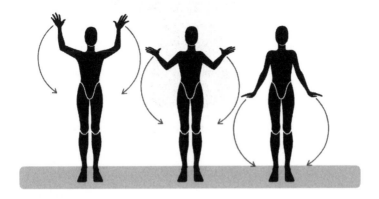

HANDS ON THE SOLAR PLEXUS

~ Place your right hand on your solar plexus and your left hand about 4in (10cm) in front of your right hand.

~ Remain in this posture for a few minutes; energy is now being supplied to the body.

~ The solar plexus relaxes and a vortex of energy is established.

~ Feel how energy flows around your hands – it can feel like dough is being wrapped around them.

~ The blocks are resolved.

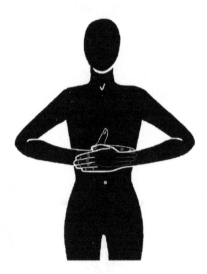

Hands on the solar plexus

CONCLUDING THE ASANAS

Finally, let your hands hang down in a relaxed state. Stand still, feel the energy, and then step backward.

With the help of the asana sequence, your body can absorb energy in a similar way to an antenna. The different positions are like different antenna shapes assigned to different frequencies. Enjoy this state, which will last for a few minutes but can also last for hours. You'll find that reactions from stressed people won't bother you and will even serve to further strengthen your own energy.

On our website, www.mindflow.academy, you'll find video instructions to help you practice the asanas daily. The video includes music that was specially composed for the asanas. I've also recorded a guide to the asanas – the recordings were made on one of our trips and show our group practicing.

PART II

MINDFLOW IN PRACTICE

Chapter 9

HOW TO ENTER G4

I should say at this point in the book that the moment you start *judging* the state of G4, you will not be able to reach it. This means that it's unwise to prepare to deal with a situation or a person by, say, using the asanas, because the expectation (judgment) of how the situation will develop is inevitably present. To enter the state of G4, you simply need to approach it with curiosity… and do what wants to be done. In this way, you're not entangled, or restricted, but are completely free.

There are various ways to reach the state of G4, and we'll explore some of them in this chapter. Experiment with the following exercises to help you reach G4 and experience it for yourself. The more often you experience G4, the easier it'll become for you to find your way into it.

Also, practice the asanas regularly (*see Chapter 8*), preferably in the morning and evening, so that the nadis for G4 energy expand and your system is strengthened and stabilized.

THE STARTING POINT

The basis of all instructions for entering G4 is as follows:

~   Relax completely and let go of your everyday thoughts and worries. Breathe calmly and deeply.

~   Free yourself from any desire, and adopt a neutral and unintentional attitude.

~   Free yourself of emotions, thoughts, and expectations about the person or situation you're currently dealing with.

~   Feel the energy flowing into you. Perceive it as a warm wind flowing into your system.

~   Enter a state of total acceptance and openness.

THE PINKIE FINGER MUDRA

Complete the exercise above before performing this exercise.

~   Place the pinkie (little) fingers of each hand together for one to two minutes; the left finger sits on top of the right. This mudra creates a kind of 'reset' of the flow of energy in your physical system. You'll become calmer and more relaxed, and can easily enter G4.

Pinkie finger mudra

THE ZERO-POINT POSITION

We described the zero-point position in Chapter 4 (*see page 81*). Return to that section and follow the instructions for performing the exercise; as you do so, notice how your gluteal muscle behaves in a relaxed state and in a tense state.

DILATION OF THE PUPILS

Follow steps 1–5 of 'The Starting Point' exercise (*see opposite*). Next, fix your gaze on a point in front of you and feel your pupils dilate – a sign that you're in G4. Practice this in front of a mirror a few times. As you'll discover, with continuous practice you'll reach G4 very quickly.

'I AM'

Say the two words 'I am' to yourself or out loud, if you're able to. This will anchor you in the here and now. You're here, unshakable and complete.

GETTING ENERGY

If you feel burned-out or lacking in energy, you can recharge your batteries at any time by using the two following exercises. Imagine they're like a jet of water being directed at you, filling up your energy system.

THE ENERGY OF A RIVER

Picture yourself walking upstream (against the flow) along the bank of a river. Imagine the energy of the water flowing into your energy system. The water will cleanse you, and the energy of the water will build your energy system.

BLOW-DRY YOUR BODY

Here's another great way to absorb energy. Using a standard ionic blow dryer or tourmaline blow dryer, let the air flow onto your body from the front; warm air is best as this contains more energy. Blow-dry your body from your feet to your head. The hot, ionized air will also resolve some energetic blocks.

However, don't blow-dry your *hair* during the exercise – there's a lot of energy in the hair, which could then be 'blown out' again!

Recognizing When You're in G4

Being in G4 requires a certain level of training – especially since the nadis, the energy channels in the body, are initially as thin as strands of hair. With increased practice, the nadis expand; at some point they can store enough energy for it to be available all day long.

You're in G4 when you stop feeling tension in your body after performing the asana sequence or the earlier exercises, and have the sensation that you've sunk 1½ft (50cm) into the ground. Dilated, and therefore relaxed, pupils also indicate that you're in G4 consciousness. Also, pay attention to your solar plexus – a soft and relaxed solar plexus is a good indication of G4.

As a lawyer, I've always done plenty of negotiating and I'm partial to sensible solutions rather than those forced with a crowbar, which please nobody, cost a lot of time and money, and get on everyone's nerves.

When I enter G4 and see where clients' energies are flowing, where blocks are located, and at which points individuals have become caught, I can sometimes speak openly with them about this. Then I can work toward a different solution – one that's a win-win situation for all parties, especially in the long term.

Chapter 10

THE ENERGY ACCEPTANCE TECHNIQUE

Energy acceptance is a process that allows you to resolve burdensome past and present situations in your life; it can also be used for relationships, projects, or problems. In the exercise that follows, you'll delve deeper into the issue that's most on your mind – choose one that triggers you often because there's a lot of energy present there – and then energy acceptance will give you the opportunity to take this energy in one go.

Please be aware that you're working in an integral system here: *Everything is connected to everything else.* If you draw energy from a situation in the past, it'll have an impact on your present, too, as well as on the people involved at that time. If you choose to deal with current problems or difficulties using the energy acceptance technique, then adopt an attitude of acceptance and open yourself up to new paths and possibilities.

HOW TO PERFORM ENERGY ACCEPTANCE

1. First, practice the asana sequence (*see pages 133–137*).

2. Next, in your home, stand in front of a white wall/picture frame/painting/ photo, or anything else onto which you can *mentally* project an image.

3. Place your left palm on your left thigh. The right hand should be perpendicular or parallel with the white wall/picture frame/painting/ photo. (The right hand is the giving hand. We use it during energy acceptance because it 'pierces' the energy block. While the left hand rests on the thigh, a cycle is created and the energy from the block flows directly into your system.)

Energy acceptance

4. Enter G4 and let go of intention. Don't try to change anything, simply accept the energy.

5. Now, project an issue that you'd like to resolve in your life onto the wall/picture frame/painting/photo, using it as a 'canvas.' Don't delve into the issue. Simply observe what's happening without being part of it. Keep your eyes open; you're merely an observer.

6. Now tap into the energy that resides in this issue for you, as if you've turned on the tap for a water tank and energy is now flowing into you from it.

7. When the energy shoots in, you'll feel a brief twitch in the body and the body may start to lurch.

8. As soon as the energy decreases again, the body will begin to twitch once more. Then you can lower your right hand, relax, and see if you want to accept anything else. If so, begin again from step 3.

9. Distribute the energy as you would as part of the asana sequence (*see page 138*).

10. When you're finished, step out to the right in a clockwise direction.

Through practicing this technique, you've removed the energy from an issue and resolved the block behind it. You don't even have to know which block it was; it's enough to get the energy flowing. The resonance that you previously generated through this block has now been resolved and you'll no longer attract problems associated with it.

EXERCISE: ATTAINING GOOD GROUNDING

People with good grounding are difficult to influence and manipulate. This exercise will help you to achieve good grounding. It can be done either standing or seated, and should be performed three times to help you gain a really good level of energy.

~ Enter G4.

~ As shown in the illustration below, direct your attention from the left big toe (1) to the right big toe (2), up to the left knee (3), then to the right knee (4), then over the root chakra, up to the head, and further up, beyond the crown chakra. Using your right hand, you can guide and support the flow of energy from 1 through 4.

~ Finally, you can accelerate the flow of energy with a sweeping, vertically shooting hand movement from the root chakra beyond the crown chakra.

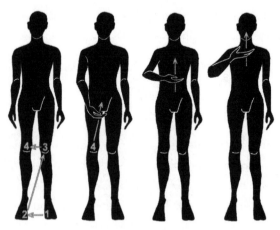

Good grounding

Immediately after the grounding exercise you may feel a flow of heat in the body, a tingling in your feet, or feel that you're sitting heavier on the chair. A word of warning: Don't cross your hands afterward, otherwise you'll cancel out the grounding.

TESTIMONIAL
Maria from Murnau, Germany

Privately and professionally, my life has changed completely since I started using MindFlow. I have a lot more energy throughout the day; I'm tired much less often; and I also know how to help myself in difficult situations.

I'm a surgeon, and when a patient comes for an initial consultation, I often already have a sense of what's missing and why they're there. I always enter G4 before performing surgery. The amazing thing is that barely any scars remain on the patients on whom I operate, and their post-operative healing process is much better and quicker. There are far fewer complications, too. I don't know how it's possible – it's just the way it is. Blocks are removed from the patient and they're able to heal themselves again.

When I enter G4, I notice how the other person changes too, as they're taken along by my energy field. They relax. In this way, certain things that are current concerns for the patient can occasionally be solved. And sometimes patients cancel their consultations because their symptoms have resolved and they no longer need an operation.

Chapter 11

LIVING IN G4

As soon as we move into a dimension that's outside of those in which one loses energy, there's automatically a gain in the level of life energy. In D9–D12, or G4, there's a permanent flow of energy toward you. And in G4 there's no time; it can expand or contract.

When you're in G4, you're in D9; here, everything is good as long as you *really are* in G4: 100% life energy! At the dimensions below that, on the other hand, you experience a permanent loss of energy. In principle, it's about returning to G4 as soon as you realize that you've fallen out of this state. And as soon as you experience a situation in which you're at somebody else's mercy, you can escape it by entering G4.

In New York a guy once attacked me and held a gun to my temple. As a Taurus, I don't like to give up, so I asked the man: 'Are you sure it works?' In that second, he lost his focus;

the moment he loosened his grip, I turned his hand so that he could no longer use it because his finger was suffering.

Whoever is attacked may take everything from the attacker; it's an invitation to teach them the lesson or to take away the block. In this case, it meant the man could at least do nothing of the sort in the near future. (But be careful, a reaction like mine isn't recommended if you're not absolutely sure that you can cope with the situation! If you aren't, it's advisable to hand over your wallet to the attacker.)

RESPONSIBILITY

As soon as you do something without intention, you'll invariably be able to take responsibility for it, as you've done it with your whole being. At this point, there's also no 'having doubts.' As soon as you receive an impulse, you also receive all the information; all the necessary people and resources will be supplied to you.

As soon as you receive information in G4, you simply know it. You then have total awareness of it; there's also no longer any external influence because in G4 you're directly located in the superior spiritual hyperspace. You have the information and you direct the energy. Everything is aligned with you.

This is the big difference. There's no right or wrong here, no sure or unsure, no better or worse. You just put it into practice, take appropriate steps, and do it. This is life in G4.

FEELINGS AND EMOTIONS

Let's go a step further. What follows may be difficult for some readers to believe, but I ask you to accept it for now. The longer you do this work, the better you'll understand the teachings.

Emotions can lead to the biggest blocks that we impose on ourselves. In a perpetrator-victim mentality, the following applies: 'I love you, so you have to love me too.' If I love a person and I don't want to lose them, I've taken possession of them.

The need for attachment ultimately arises from deprivation, and the resulting fear of losing someone and being alone. But ideally, it would be something more akin to this quotation from the novel *Wilhelm Meister's Apprenticeship* by Johann Wolfgang von Goethe: '... and if I love you, what is it to you?' Both people are allowed to exist, and both are allowed to exist *as they are*. From this, something wonderful develops – without dependency and co-dependency.

I once coached a newly enamored couple with attachment issues: She didn't want to commit, but he clung on. I suggested they just stay together for a day. Then another day, and another day after that. They've now been together for 28 years.

It is important to distinguish between feelings and emotions. Feelings tend to be experienced consciously and expressed verbally, while emotions originate in the subconscious (in the limbic system, the most primitive area of the brain) and then manifest on a psycho-physiological level, enabling conscious or unconscious emotional experiences. The Latin root word of emotion (*exmovere*) means to 'move out from' or 'stir up,' referencing the idea that emotions arise from a deeper area of the brain.

Emotions are accompanied by a judgment and are triggered by expectations and experiences, hopes and fears – for example, the fear of losing one's partner – which, in the case of negatively experienced emotions, can lead to blocks.

SHIFTING YOUR FOCUS

Now we'll go a little bit deeper. Something is considered 'bad luck' when, according to our judgment, it went wrong, since we like to 'play God' and want to control everything. It's important to understand that everything is 'equally relevant' – 'equal relevance' has the same value.

Translated into G4, we could say: 'I'm getting what I deserve because I can accept it.' By implication, when it comes to 'bad luck,' this means, for example, that something or someone has left because I no longer need it/her/him. It's no longer relevant for me because now something else will acquire the same relevance.

However, since many people get stuck in the emotions of grief and loss at this point, they can't accept the other relevant thing. Their focus continues to dwell on the loss and grief. The lasting feeling of love for another person is always there, it will never pass; love is lasting and it connects.

We must remember that there's no victim-perpetrator thinking in G4. You can't be at a higher level and feel like a perpetrator or a victim; this is mutually incompatible because then you'd be handing over responsibility.

Some of my seminar participants struggle at this particular point, as they're suddenly unable to continue playing their role as the victim. One young man had neither hands nor arms, but I showed him that, in spite of this, his hands were still energetically present. His father, who was also at the seminar, collapsed during an exercise, as it was *he* who had the block, not his son. The son is now completely relaxed; with the help of prostheses, he's learned to drive a car, and he's abandoned his victim role. He realized that he's capable of doing everything possible and that he's responsible for his life.

HEALTH

When you're in G4, your body automatically becomes healthy; cells regenerate themselves. Many of my seminar participants who've been using the MindFlow Method for some time now feel more vital and actually look younger and stronger. This is because diseases are just disturbances and blocks in the energy system, which dissolve in G4.

CONFLICT SITUATIONS

As a person in G4, you'll also encounter conflict. So, how do you deal with conflict when you're acting without intention and without desire? First of all, it's always important to enter G4, to energetically commit to your true greatness and to build yourself up in this sense. You acknowledge your true self. In this situation, you can say, silently: 'I am,' and then just see what happens.

At this point I want to tell you a story that illustrates this. We had to renovate the roof of our house, so the place was a building site for a long time. At some point, our neighbor said that it was all too much for him; he found the upheaval irritating. One afternoon my wife came home briefly to check on the work, and our neighbor ran beside her as she did so, complaining about our 'No Parking' signs, and wanting to know if the whole thing was official.

Before long, the police were standing in our garden. We were able to clarify everything, provide information about how we'd acquired the 'No Parking' signs, and so on. Afterward I went over to our neighbor's house and asked him directly: 'Did you call the police?' Of course, he had to admit to it. I said to him: '*You* are very difficult. You fight with all the neighbors. But why? Guess what? I'm also going to be difficult now. From today onward, I'm going to be a real pain.'

With that statement I mirrored my neighbor's behavior from a G4 position. And that was it. Since then we've never had any trouble or conflict with him. I stayed in G4, engaged him with his own energetic position, showed him how it feels to be like that, and in this way, resolved his block. We now have a 'normal' relationship.

SENSITIVE PEOPLE

As you now know, the person with less energy always attacks the one with more energy. What you also need to know is that sensitive people have a lot of energy by their very nature. They're on a higher energy level because they can 'read' a lot into things, i.e. perceive a lot and gain information from this. Therefore, they have a problem in that many people draw on them and want something from them.

The boss unconsciously chooses the sensitive employees, the balancing ones, in order to fill their own low energy level, because it's easy to take energy from these particular employees. The boss wouldn't turn to someone who has less energy, because there's nothing there for them to get. They reprimand and criticize, and 'bend' the sensitive, balancing employee who is sitting there in shock. The reaction is immediate – the energy has flowed. The boss has gained energy. Will they return for more? Yes, it's highly likely.

All those whom you think have power over you and have everything under control – while you yourself, as a sensitive person, don't know how to ask for a little help – are actually weakened and want to draw energy from somewhere else. Particularly sensitive people, those who are easily stressed and who constantly think that they can no longer stand it all – the people around them, their job, problems with their partner, and so on – can benefit from MindFlow.

TRAUMA

Traumatized people have stashed away an enormous amount of energy in a way that's comparable to a water tank. Once they start using the appropriate technique, the 'water' floats over them – the trauma is gone. When the cause is gone, the effect also disappears; the cause is energetically resolved.

Visits to the dentist are a source of great fear for many people; simply lying down in the dentist's chair evokes emotions of helplessness. One dentist tried to cure her anxious patients by putting on a red nose or the like, but that tactic didn't work because it resonated with the patients' fears and tended to make them worse.

When I trained this dentist, along with her practice team, in MindFlow, I advised her to let the drill roar and say to the patient: 'Darn, I forgot my glasses! But don't worry, it'll be fine.' Sometimes she appeared in front of the patient in a blood-spattered gown, saying: 'The last treatment was really bad!' Of course, she had to learn to master the technique. There's no point just teasing… and then going under.

TESTIMONIAL
Thomas from Munich, Germany

My son Maximilian is almost in his mid-twenties and has a disability. He was the trigger for me to set out and begin searching. Due to Maximilian's situation, I fell into a deep hole, into feelings of guilt, and this eventually resulted in the breakup of my marriage. My goal has always been to find a way to communicate with my son.

As a premature baby, Maximilian had a third-degree brain bleed, and as a result, he can't speak or walk; he's fully dependent on care, and he has to be fed. But he's so optimistic, and he shines! He lives in the here and now. When I work on him with the MindFlow Method, and look him in the eye, I can see immediately how he responds to it. He's made great strides since we began – he's softened. I have the impression that he's come out of himself more. The care supervisors who work with him are now all happy and balanced.

Chapter 12

THE POWER TOOL

In this chapter we'll explore a technique that I like to refer to in my seminars as 'the power tool.' I call it this to make us realize that with it, we really can influence our reality. First of all, I'll give you some information on how to use the power tool.

BLOCKS AND RESONANCE

As I've said several times previously, *everyone* has blocks. In fact, some people even like to acquire new blocks on a regular basis, often at the same time that others have been resolved; they're used to these blocks – their bodies are virtually emotionally addicted to them! An illness, for example, is the result of an accumulation of energy in the lower three dimensions and in time, i.e. in D1–D4. If the illness is cured but the energetic block behind it remains, the illness can manifest itself again at any time.

The more blocks you have, the fewer freedoms you have. As long as you have blocks, you have your hands closed, metaphorically speaking, because they're desperately holding on to something else. But with closed hands you can't accept anything that's available to you. To be able to receive, you first have to open your hands.

Another problem with blocks is your *resonance* with the related issues (*see Chapter 5, page 91*). When you're afraid of something, you wear it on the outside and so your fear is always being confirmed. We call this *stress resonance*. The resonance will only disappear when this fear is eliminated and you're no longer confronted with the issue in question.

But how do you get around this limitation? The solution is amazingly simple: by Not-Wanting! In doing something that serves no purpose – that is, something that's not done 'in order to…' – the mind can regain its freedom and blocks are resolved. Consider how much of what you do is connected to an 'in order to…'!

The trick, therefore, is to remove blocks in a higher dimension. The higher the dimension, the more forcefully and effectively the block can be resolved. In the best case, it will be 'so far up' that it can't reappear – similar to weeds that need to be grabbed and pulled out at the roots. Being free means being able to accept the possibilities offered to you by G4. With MindFlow, you learn to work with your own existence. Not-Doing with existence…

Here's an example based on a D4 block problem. If we're under time pressure, we're permanently losing energy. Furthermore, who is it who gains energy when we're pressed for time and someone with whom we have an appointment is deliberately late? The other person!

In my time in the armed forces, the curfew was at 10 p.m.; we had to travel on Sunday evenings to get there on time. My best friend was one of those people who always turned up late, sometimes even two hours late. I played along several times and got myself all worked up, until one Sunday evening I left five minutes after our scheduled 7 p.m. appointment, even though he arrived at 7:07 p.m. From that moment on he was on time! I didn't want to annoy him; however, I stopped reinforcing his actions and his block, and I did something with my whole existence – and therefore there were no repercussions.

CHANGING REALITY – THE MAGNET

Let's turn this train of thought around. You could create an energy that in turn creates a different kind of resonance, a *desired resonance*, in your life. But be careful because there's a danger in doing this: In the process you must not adopt an attitude of 'wanting' or 'having to do' something! You just raise your hand, so to speak – which in G4 shows that you're ready for an experience or a creation in your life.

So it's *not* about *wanting*, but about *acceptance and openness!* Understanding this difference is very important. That which you're ready to accept, rather than that which you want, will come to you. This is a major difference from many other techniques.

Feel it! Be certain that 'it' has already occurred. Now the only thing left to do is to receive. It goes without saying that it comes to you because you're already living it. If, for example, you want to create abundance and wealth through professional success, the readiness to do so would be: *I'm successful in my job and consequently gain abundance and wealth in my life.*

Really *feel* this readiness! Go inside yourself and find out what triggers this readiness in you. Are there any places in your body that start to twitch? Which put up resistance? Feel exactly where there are still blocks, and release those blocks with the energy acceptance technique (*see page 152*).

USING THE POWER TOOL

I'd like to introduce you to working with the power tool by using a concrete example. Imagine you want to create a life partnership based on love, understanding, and well-meaning cooperation – everything you'd suppose a successful life partnership to be.

Here's what to do:

1. First, enter the G4 consciousness.

2. Next, create a 'magnet.' To do this, imagine that you're raising your hand in G4, in the knowledge and firm conviction that you're *already* in a loving partnership with another person. You have this partnership *already*, *now*. There's no desire and no intention behind it. It's also not something that will happen in the future, but something that already exists in this moment. Be aware that it's already occurred, and then it will be delivered to you.

3. Express your readiness: 'I have a loving partnership. I accept it because it's already occurred.'

4. Allow the feeling that you associate with your partnership to flow out of you, constantly, everywhere, no matter where you are.

You've now created a magnet. In time, you'll encounter this partnership – be open to it as it presents itself to you. But above all, you'll be in total acceptance! It's also possible that a previous partnership will change as a result and develop to this level. Or the previous partnership may crumble. Everything is possible and all paths are open. You can't influence how something comes to you and the path it chooses. Nor do you need to worry about it. The only certainty is that it will come.

USING ACCELERATORS

Now you can also work with accelerators, which increase your energy and, as a result, the energy of your magnet. The more energy you have, the stronger your magnet and the faster your creation will manifest. There are many ways to accelerate; I only mention one here. Once you understand the principle, you can adapt it for yourself.

Go to a place in which crowds gather; somewhere filled with energy (for example, a football stadium). Just stand there. Go into the G4 consciousness and hold your right hand forward, as in the energy acceptance technique (*see page 152*). Your left hand should be lying on your thigh. Feel the warm wind and the way the energy circulates in your system.

Every person in G3 serves as an energy supplier for you. The greater their blocks or aggressions, the more energy and support you can get, and the stronger your magnet will become. You advance from D8–D9 (possibly even to D10 or above). At some point your creation will be so 'far up' that everything aligns itself to this creation and thus it happens or fulfills itself.

And it gets even better: The higher your energy rises, the more energy you can receive directly from G4. Note that it's *not about being in the state of wanting*, but in *total acceptance of what's coming*. In my seminars I like to explain this using the following image: First, you sow the seed of a tree (create a magnet), and then the seed germinates. Energy flows through the release of blocks and the absorption of collective energy; this corresponds to watering the tree. The tree continues to grow. At some point it's able to take care of itself because the roots have become strong and have spread.

This corresponds to the permanent inflow of energy from G4. This is exactly what happens once you're in D9 or above. Then there's nothing left to do, no more watering or fertilizing. It happens and becomes real.

TESTIMONIAL
Betina from Magdeburg, Germany

Before I started working with MindFlow, I walked through life with a sense of enjoyment and happiness, but the handbrake was always on. As a result, I became a typical worrywart and always considered every eventuality. My fears were as much a part of my life as my daily bread – they included existential dread, fear of dogs, fear of the dentist, and so on.

I'd worked on all my programming from the past a thousand times, and I realize now that it had held me back over the course of my life; it affected everything – family, job, health, finances. Stress raged in me like water boiling in a saucepan.

Since familiarizing myself with MindFlow, I've been able to look at my life from a completely new perspective, without judging or convicting myself. It's really relaxing. I've incorporated many of the techniques I've learned into my everyday life and they're easy to practice – I don't have to *do* anything.

My thinking is completely new; my thoughts are quieter, more mindful, and more peaceful toward myself. I've been able to stop my medication for high blood pressure and a rapid heartbeat. I can ask questions now, and ask for help, support, and ideas. Most of the time the door opens the moment I do this. I go to work feeling relaxed, and I sleep well once more. I'm taking better and better care of myself, and I'm doing well. I laugh a lot more, too. Of course, there was a 'hole' as well as concerns and fear, but now I have a lot more life energy and zest for life. I say with a wink that 'MindFlow saved my backside.'

Appendix

MINDFLOW FOR BUSINESS

In a business setting the MindFlow Method gives us the opportunity to remain consistently relaxed and not respond to announcements from customers or bosses that could upset us. As a result, we stay calm and can keep a clear head in every situation. We can do our job and achieve better results if we keep our energy. Here's how it works:

Resolving Tensions in the Workplace

Usually, tensions arise at work because everyone is stressed and has to achieve their goals; at this point you lose energy. Tensions with colleagues arise from expectations that can't be met by the other person – or when you can't meet your own expectations. You can release this stress by entering G4 and saying to yourself: *Fine, there are no expectations at all – nevertheless, I will achieve my goals.*

Resolving Tensions with Your Boss

Due to a heavy workload and a high level of responsibility, our superiors tend to be notoriously tired and exhausted. This means that they often approach employees who have more energy than they do in order to gain energy from them. If *you* are this employee, then you should be aware that the boss is coming to you of all people because you have more energy than they do. With this knowledge, you can relax and wait and see what the boss wants from you.

If you're the boss, and are experiencing tensions with an employee because you notice they're not performing and are drawing energy from you, it may be because your management style is very 'giving,' allowing the employee to rest on their laurels and let you do their job. It's important to counteract this. Set a deadline for the employee, and if that doesn't work, you should act consistently and hire a new person for the position.

Creating Harmonious Interaction at Work

Harmony doesn't mean giving others a free pass all the time, but rather being in balance. Those who are in balance won't have extreme 'outbursts.' It's easy for employees or colleagues to assess you when you're in balance; you're reliable, the work is done in a relaxed manner and finished without stress. If every employee knows how to interact with mutual trust, it's perfect. Then the team works independently, effectively, and without stress.

MindFlow for Sales Talks: How to Sell Better

Focusing on selling isn't the right approach here. If you're convinced by your company's product, you can respond to every objection to it made by your counterpart by saying internally, over and over again, *That's allowed*. Doing so will result in your counterpart becoming calmer and having the opportunity to remove their blocks related to your offer. Once the blocks are no longer there, why wouldn't they buy your product?

MindFlow for Greater Business Efficiency

To me, inefficiency means that a lot of energy is wasted in the process. If everyone in the company is familiar with G4 and trained in it, the employee who isn't a good fit for the company will be the first to go; the other employees will then be more relaxed and can take care of their work instead of group processes.

Averting a Crisis or Bankruptcy

A crisis can be seen as what it is – a situation that's allowed to exist. As soon as the person concerned realizes that this situation is completely okay, they can suddenly emerge from their tension and find solutions. Bankruptcy is often no longer necessary.

Cash Flow and Skillful Money Handling

Money is always an expression of your own attitude toward energy; having little money therefore means that you like to waste energy on others. Increase your energy level, and money 'has to' follow because energy-rich people are also rich in money!

QUESTIONS AND ANSWERS

While you're reading this book and engaging with the MindFlow Method, as well as implementing it in practice, a few questions are bound to arise – perhaps one of the following:

Q: How can I practice absorbing stress energy from others?

Test it at home with your partner or with friends. Let yourself be insulted or confronted with allegations, and then adopt this attitude: *I gave the other person the task of doing this to me. They're allowed to do this!* The moment you feel a little 'jolt' in your body or muscle tone, or when you feel warmth, you're absorbing energy.

Q: Through practicing MindFlow, will I become more receptive to energies from the astral plane? Can I learn to see auras or come into contact with spiritual beings?

In G4 you have no contact with spiritual beings. These kinds of meetings take place in G3. You can learn to see auras, of course, but in G3, rather than in G4.

Q: Does black or white magic exist?

Black and white magic take place in G3 and work with G3 techniques, i.e. techniques of manipulation. These aren't applicable in G4 where they're ineffective.

Q: Can I treat specific diseases using MindFlow?

Doctors treat diseases. However, in G4, you can relax your body so that it functions without tension. You have to imagine it as follows: Muscle tension is very painful, and the sooner the body lets go, the easier it is for the tension to disappear. There's no tension in G4, neither on a physical nor a psychological level. Someone in G4 doesn't treat themselves at all, because that would be goal-oriented behavior. Instead, they enter G4 and allow the body to work and regenerate itself. After all, none of us evolved from baby to adult on purpose; it just happened – in G4.

Q: Is there such a thing as 'distance healing'? For example, can I send energy to another person from G4 even if he's not close to me?

When I want to transfer energy, it happens in a goal-oriented way. These are G3 techniques that have nothing to do with G4.

CONCLUSION

Dear readers,

The MindFlow Method, and the tools you've learned in this book, can accompany you for a lifetime. When does a tree stop growing? When it dies. Seen in this way, your life and your *mind* are always in flow, in a steady flow.

Having read this book, you've opened the door to a new system – and the whole universe behind it. I, and the teachers trained by me, teach further and more in-depth exercises, as well as treatment techniques, in seminars and training courses; during these, participants learn more about how to resolve blocks and how to help people gain more freedom as a result. We also offer MindFlow sessions: a treatment with one of the MindFlow experts we've trained. With MindFlow and G4, as with so much in life, practice makes perfect.

However you proceed with your MindFlow journey, I'd like to keep in touch with you. You're welcome to subscribe to our newsletter, where, as a gift, you'll receive a video with beautiful background music that you can use for daily practice of the asanas. We use the newsletter to inform you about everything that's happening related to MindFlow. You'll also find seminar and training dates and a list of experts; you'll find the registration form for the newsletter at www.mindflow.academy.

I wish you a life in flow!

Yours,

Tom Moegele

THANK YOU!

I'd like to thank the many people without whom this book would never have been created, especially my wife, who has always motivated me to share my experiences with my readers. Thanks to Aunt Emma, Lil, and Val for the crazy ideas.

I'm very lucky to meet and work with new and valuable people every day, and for that, I'm very grateful. I'd like to bow to them and say: THANK YOU!

WORKING WITH
TOM MOEGELE

Visit www.mindflow.academy to find dates and detailed information about the following seminars.

MindFlow Basis Seminar

In this seminar, participants learn to work with their own energy, to hold it, and to increase it. Through working in a large group activation, participants' energy levels are raised to an elevated state of consciousness, the G4 consciousness. Using physical exercises, an understanding of their own energy is intensified. Participants learn to resolve blocks, and as a result, achieve internal freedom. Be ready to accept everything for your life!

MindFlow Practitioner

Prerequisite: MindFlow basis seminar

The MindFlow practitioner training comprises three weekend seminars. In this training block, participants become active users of G4 consciousness and learn how to passively and actively de-stress their fellow human beings and thus release their blocks. They also learn effective response patterns to attacks and how to use their energy to always remain one step ahead of a counterpart.

MindFlow Expert

Prerequisite: MindFlow basis seminar and MindFlow practitioner

In this intensive workshop spanning three weekends, participants learn effective treatment techniques in order to work with clients. These include realigning the client's energy system to remove blocks and implants, and to put the client in a G4-like state in which they can accept what they long for in life. They also learn how to travel with the mind to release energetic blocks that have settled in the upper dimensions.

- Graduation with a certificate and a license as a MindFlow Expert

- Inclusion in our expert list at www.mindflow.academy

As a MindFlow Expert, you are able to offer expert treatment sessions for a fixed fee per session. Find out more at: www.mindflow.academy.

Online Course: 'System Reset'

In this online course, participants learn to resolve their blocks and tensions fully, in order to gain their own energy and freedom. The 'system reset' accompanies the participant over 12 weeks with a daily five-minute exercise that will affect changes in the entire body system.

- 12 exercises; one new exercise every week

- Each exercise lasts 5 minutes maximum and is carried out once or twice a day

The 'system reset' course offers lifetime access: You can view the videos as often as you wish, without limits, and can start the course at any time. Find more information at: www. mindflow.academy.

ABOUT THE AUTHOR

Katharina Renter, Munich

Tom Moegele is an author, speaker, and the creator of the MindFlow Method. He became aware of his clairvoyant abilities as a child but repressed them in order to fit in. After a career in investment banking in London, he developed his revolutionary method, known as MindFlow – a new understanding of stress, anxiety, and emotional blocks as doorways to an infinite source of life energy.

Tom now offers private coaching sessions and leads seminars and workshops in Germany and internationally.

www.mindflow.academy

HAY HOUSE

Look within

Join the conversation about latest products, events, exclusive offers and more.

f   Hay House

🐦   @HayHouseUK

📷   @hayhouseuk

❤️   healyourlife.com

We'd love to hear from you!